The Greatest of GREAT ESCAPES

The Greatest of GREAT ESCAPES

Rotherham United's Finest Hour

Holly Hunt

pitch

First published by Pitch Publishing, 2025

Pitch Publishing
9 Donnington Park,
85 Birdham Road,
Chichester,
West Sussex,
PO20 7AJ
www.pitchpublishing.co.uk
info@pitchpublishing.co.uk

A CIP catalogue record is available for this book from the British Library.

ISBN 978 1 80150 944 2

MIX
Paper | Supporting responsible forestry
FSC™ C016779

Printed and bound on FSC® certified paper in line with our continuing commitment to ethical business practices, sustainability and the environment.

Typesetting and origination by Pitch Publishing

Printed and bound in India by Replika Press Pvt. Ltd.

Contents

Foreword

IT DOESN'T come easy, being a Rotherham United fan. There's never any middle ground and I think that sums up how Rotherham are always trying to bridge that gap between League One and the Championship. It's hard to do, but the Championship is interesting to watch every season – there is always something to play for somewhere in every game, which is what you want as fans.

It's fine margins – you don't want to be mediocre and have a season where there's nothing happening. It's a very hard balance to get but in the seasons where we managed to stay up, we had a proper go at it, like that year in 2015/16. That season is something that will go down in history. All Rotherham fans remember that season as much as the promotions and the good times that we've had.

I've had some bad times at Rotherham, but that made the highs even higher. When I look back, because I've had that many highs, they far outweigh the lows. They go hand-in-hand. I wouldn't have had so many high points if I hadn't had the low points.

I loved every minute of my time at the club, even the bad times for me personally. And I probably wouldn't have been at Rotherham still if not for Neil Warnock; he's one of a kind. Up until that point during that season when he was appointed as the new manager, I knew my time at Rotherham was probably over and that's how I felt.

I'd been out on loan and not in favour, but that all changed when Neil Warnock came in and gave me confidence. He knew what I was all about and he trusted me. That's how he got the best out of me.

Towards the end of that season, everybody thought we were down and out. That's why the fans took to me so much. I know what's required and I know what it's like at that sort of club. It's about being hard-working and giving everything. I don't mess about, I get stuck in and I give it a proper go, which is all Rotherham fans want to see.

I've been written off so many times by different managers, fans and various players – everybody really – and if I get written off, I want to prove them wrong. That's the mentality I've always had and I've done it so many times. I don't give up; I'll work as hard as I can and prove people wrong and that sums up my Rotherham career. It's always been like that. For the nine years I was at the club, it was the same mentality everybody had and I embraced that and used it as motivation in the right way.

With promotions, play-off finals and winning cups, you get the trophy and you walk up the steps and get the accolade of showing it off, but fighting off relegation, you don't get a trophy to show for it. However, it was the same elation and the same celebrations. It's similar emotions.

It was miraculous, how we did it in that short space of time from nowhere under Warnock and it goes down as a highlight alongside the promotions I've had with the club. It was a big achievement for Rotherham, especially under the circumstances. We were the underdogs – everybody had written us off.

You don't think about that outside negativity at the time – you just roll on to the next game and we were on the crest of a wave. We were just digging in for each other, playing well and grinding out results. Everything seemed to go our way. The momentum and the atmosphere around the place was unbelievable. As soon as Neil walked through the door, the change was refreshing. He had the respect of everyone straight away and that's how you build teams.

It's only when you look back now and look at what we did that you think 'Wow!' It doesn't happen often. Teams don't go on a run like that out of nowhere, especially when you're at the bottom of the Championship and struggling. I hope that fans look back on that season for years to come – and they should do. I definitely will because I can't see something like that happening again.

It will be reflected on for years and I'm sure, in years to come, there will be legends nights – maybe with Neil Warnock, other players who were involved and myself – and reunions where fans assemble and look back on the time that we spent together.

It's crazy how quickly time passes and it's almost been a decade since the start of that campaign. This book will be a nice memento to fondly remember those times in words and reimagine it again to get people talking about it. I remember the games and what went on but there are still little details that catch my imagination again. I'm sure this book will put a smile on Rotherham fans' faces.

Nobody can say we were lucky or it was a fluke. We worked hard, we grafted and it paid off. It was just a pleasure to be a part of. How we ended up surviving that season, due to Neil Warnock coming in and going on that ridiculous run, sums up us as a club and the mentality and togetherness that we had. That's why Rotherham fans look back on it fondly and I'm sure many people will never forget that season.

If you ask every player, the manager and the chairman, it really was the great escape.

Richard Wood

Prologue

CORNWALL. WITH its golden sandy beaches and picturesque coastlines, tucked away in its own tranquil corner of the country, those that have paid a visit to the idyllic South West of England will know that it's almost feasible to imagine you are somewhere in the Mediterranean, perhaps, without even having to step foot on an aeroplane. Picture this: you're relaxing by the ocean, soaking in the sounds of the waves rhythmically lapping at the shore on a warm summer's evening. It makes you ask yourself: why, should you have the choice, would you ever want to leave a place like that?

You might appreciate, then, why legendary football boss Neil Warnock opted to pack up his life and relocate there with his wife, Sharon. After falling in love with the area and purchasing a property whilst Neil was in charge of Plymouth Argyle between 1995 and 1997, the couple made the move before Warnock took a hiatus from his management career – a break which many translated into his unofficial P45. How wrong they were.

Having been out of work since December 2014 – aside from a temporary stint in the dugout with Queens Park Rangers – when he departed Crystal Palace, it was going to take a lot to tempt him back up to South Yorkshire when the call came in from another of his former clubs, Rotherham United. Settled in his new life away from the limelight, it took a quiet word from Sharon to eventually win her husband over.

It's fair to say that football isn't the most popular sport in Warnock's spiritual home near Stoke Climsland – a village on Cornwall's rural eastern border – and the wider county. As well as rugby, surfing and other water-based activities – for obvious reasons – are preferred over football, although you can still find a handful of non-league and semi-professional teams, from Falmouth Town to Truro City, scattered across the region.

That meant Rotherham had an ace up their sleeve. They had the one thing Cornwall didn't: a football club in crisis. Warnock could only ignore the SOS from Millers chairman Tony Stewart for so long before he took him up on his offer. The situation in which the club found themselves had struck a chord. So, on 11 February 2016, Warnock was officially unveiled as the new Rotherham manager on a short-term deal until the end of the season as he made the 600-mile round trip up to his native South Yorkshire – a journey he would become familiar with during his time with the club. And although that might sound like the hard part, it most certainly wasn't. In fact, it was an uphill battle which had only just begun.

Warnock, who was born and raised in neighbouring Sheffield, had his work cut out for him this time. Rotherham were destined for the drop. By the time the new boss was three games into his tenure, the club were six points adrift of safety in the Championship with just 13 fixtures remaining to save themselves before the curtain came down on the 2015/16 campaign. The Millers had already been through two managers in the space of five months and were hoping the third time was a charm. It simply had to be.

For a club that had enjoyed plenty of success in the years leading up to Warnock's arrival – winning back-to-back promotions which charted a course from League Two to the Championship between 2012 and 2014, ending their nine-year exile from the second tier of English football – they had been brought back down to earth with a thud. The harsh reality of just how difficult it would be to compete was sinking in as they attempted to go toe-to-toe with some of the division's giants. Before a ball had even been kicked to get the campaign under way, it had already been decided by many that Rotherham would struggle once again. There was nothing new there. After all, they had just about managed to survive in 2014/15, despite being hit with a points deduction late in the day. Few outsiders were surprised to see the Millers treading water once again, but they would soon sit up and take notice when they saw the near unfathomable course of events unfolding right in front of their very eyes.

Fortunately for Rotherham, the Championship was Warnock's bread and butter. He and the division were old acquaintances and the new Rotherham boss was more than familiar with the cut and thrust of the league. Three of his seven promotions had come in the second tier, with Notts County, Sheffield United and QPR. But Rotherham weren't making a bid for a top-six finish. Instead, they were anxiously glancing over their shoulder. The finish line drew nearer with each game that sucked them further into a relegation dogfight. It would be a new challenge for Warnock, too, who was used to looking up rather than down.

There were no great expectations and perhaps that was one of the contributing factors to the cause. It had been a miserable season thus far and a cursory glance at the final run-in didn't exactly breed confidence. If Rotherham had already (and fairly recently) been outclassed by their three biggest relegation rivals – MK Dons, Charlton Athletic and Bolton Wanderers – what chance did they have of taking points from the league's high-flyers?

Nobody quite knew how the remaining months of the season would unfold but they did know that they would have no choice but to at least give it their best go with Warnock now at the helm. Would the new boss be rusty or would he be well rested and ready for action? Rotherham were a team that had lost their way – all but ready to wave the white flag. It wasn't just the fans who had abandoned the last remaining sliver of hope they were desperately clinging on to, either – it was seemingly the players, too. But where everyone else saw doom and gloom, Warnock saw a chance to make history. He saw experienced heads where others saw lost causes. He saw a chance for his players to redeem themselves where others saw 1,440 minutes of football to go through the motions. He saw a glass half full where others saw it drained and empty. That 'can do' attitude would be the bedrock in the fight to avoid falling through the trapdoor.

All of the fundamentals were in place for the boss to make a success of his return to the dugout. He had the characters, he had the backing of the club's chief and he had a fanbase willing to give him the benefit of the doubt, despite harbouring their own reservations about whether he could really pull it off. He had proved before that he could succeed on a shoestring. All he needed to do was give everyone something to feed off – a positive result on the pitch to rekindle the pipe dream of extending the club's stay in the Championship, a level they had worked so hard to reach. Not to mention that the former winger had spent time on the club's books as a player. So Warnock knew what it meant to wear the red and white of Rotherham. He had the tools at his disposal, but it was more a matter of whether he had enough time to turn it around. Nobody needed reminding that that particular commodity was very much of the essence. These were the burning questions that needed answering, and fast.

Impossible wasn't a word that Warnock had space for in his vocabulary, but frustration and exasperation were very much a part of Rotherham supporters' repertoire, especially given the season they had witnessed. Nothing had been decided. Their fate wasn't mathematically sealed but, as each day passed, belief seeped away and the situation was as dismal as it had ever been. The Millers failed to see where their next win might come from.

Nevertheless, there was still life in both Rotherham United and Neil Warnock. It would be a tough ask but if, together, they did manage to pull off some kind of miracle, it would surely be an achievement worth chronicling in years to come – perhaps in a book. One thing was for sure, the great escape was well and truly on.

Chapter One

Reset and Refresh

NO SOONER had Rotherham United beaten Reading 2-1 at the New York Stadium in their penultimate game of 2014/15 to secure their place in the Championship for another year, than a new season was dawning. It was a new season which brought with it fresh hopes, dreams and expectations. And after getting through their first year back in the second tier of English football – with a minor hitch – there was a sneaking suspicion that the Millers might just be able to make a go of it this time around.

Manager Steve Evans took in the moment out on the balcony at the club's shiny 12,000-seater home, which was close to full capacity on that memorable evening as he addressed a mass of red-and-white-shirted supporters in the wake of a victory over the Royals which clinched survival with a game to spare. There were scenes reminiscent of the Millers' play-off semi-final second leg triumph over Preston North End a year earlier when fans spilled on to the pitch after Evans's men booked a date at Wembley, where they would go on to seal promotion under the famous arch in the League One play-off final. The feeling this time was just as good, if not better.

But before the Scotsman hit the fancy dress shops to purchase a sombrero and a pair of colourful board shorts for the trip to Elland Road on the final day of the season (more on that later), he issued one final Braveheart-esque rallying cry, telling Sky Sports after the win: 'They can take our points, but they will never take our fighting spirit and passion to stay in the division.'

Realistically, supporters of the club were under no illusions that it was likely to be more of the same the following year. As the division's newcomers in the summer of 2014, it was almost inevitable that Rotherham would be earmarked as favourites for relegation, but it was much more than that. Punching above their weight might have just about summed it up – taking into account various different factors, from finances to facilities – but nobody could call into question their merit as a Championship club. Rotherham had earned their place in the division and it had been a long road back. If the previous 12 months had taught the fans anything, it was that their team weren't going down without a fight. The league's so-called minnows could still be the masters of their own destiny if they put their heart and soul into it. They had already proven as much. Equally, they knew only too well how to be the architects of their own downfall, as they almost were on more than one occasion over the course of the impending 2015/16 campaign.

Dull moments in the club's recent history have been few and far between, from the highs of a double promotion to the lows of battling the drop. The concept of a 'yo-yo club' has become universally accepted in football. So much so that the majority of countries have their own equivalent terminology. Rotherham so often find themselves shoehorned into that category. There might be few guarantees in football but those supporters waiting in line to pick up their season tickets or awaiting their arrival in the post could be assured that the 2015/16 season would be another entertaining one, whatever the outcome. Rotherham were no humdrum football club.

Indeed, Rotherham were a club who had enjoyed some good times in the second tier in seasons gone by. In 1954/55, they came as close as they have ever done to reaching the promised land. After recording their highest-ever league finish the season prior, they went one better the following term, placing third in the old Division Two standings. By October, the club were sitting pretty at the top of the table, only to be knocked off their perch following defeat to Liverpool at Anfield. They dusted themselves off, winning seven games on the spin as the season came to a close and, with just two games remaining, the Millers needed four points to see them promoted to the top flight.

Come the end of the campaign, the club were tied on points with nearest challengers and eventual champions Birmingham City and runners-up Luton Town. The Millers missed out on goal average. They had scored more goals than both the Blues and the Hatters, their tally of 94 surpassing Birmingham's 92 and Luton's 88. It was a bitter pill to swallow.

Fast forward some 60 years and, despite spending large parts of the 2014/15 campaign – particularly towards a nervy, latter half of the season – with their fingers, toes and everything else crossed, the Millers were seemingly a club on the up once again.

It had been a decade of peaks and troughs for the Millers, who had been relegated from the newly rebranded Championship at the end of the 2004/05 season. They finished rock bottom, where they had spent most of the season, of the second tier, 21 points short of safety. After registering just five wins in 46 league games, former manager Ronnie Moore eventually departed.

Struggles on and off the field ensued as the club's very existence hung in the balance and supporters fought to save Rotherham United. The Millers twice went into administration before they were exiled from the town following a dispute with their former landlord. Instructed to return to Rotherham within four years under the stipulations set out by the football authorities, they vacated and moved to Don Valley Stadium in Sheffield. The sporting venue – where Olympic gold medallist Jessica Ennis-Hill used to train – had a pitch which was separated from the spectator stands by an athletics track which ran the circumference of the stadium. The chasm, both physically and metaphorically, deepened as they faced an uncertain future. But a lot can change in ten years and the Millers rose from the ashes.

A change of ownership saw local businessman Tony Stewart give the club a new lease of life. After eventually returning to the town to christen the newly constructed New York Stadium, the club achieved back-to-back promotions, sending the Millers shooting back up from League Two to the Championship. Evans, the man who would lead the club into battle in 2015/16, had given the fanbase something to cheer about once again.

* * *

With pre-season on the horizon and the 2015/16 campaign fast approaching, Rotherham boss Evans had a figure in mind of how many new recruits he wanted to bring to the club as he plotted his course of action for the upcoming transfer window. The Scotsman, who said he had already identified a handful of key targets, revealed he hoped to bring in 'six or seven' permanent signings. He also admitted that he had perhaps overused the loan market in 2014/15, with the club bringing in 19 players on temporary deals over the course of the campaign. It was an honest and frank assessment from Evans.

'We want permanent signings in the main. We recognise that we brought in too many loan signings last season, but sometimes you have to bring them in to cover for injury or just to make us stronger,' he told the club's official website at the beginning of June. 'Of course, everyone understands that when you're Rotherham United and you go into the Championship level, it's fantastic for us all, but the task gets harder for Paul Douglas [chief operating officer] in terms of getting players over the line and agreeing the finances.'

On paper, the Rotherham manager was building a squad with an ideal blend of experienced heads and youthful spirit. Aidy White was one of Evans's first signings. The left-sided player arrived from Leeds United, where he came through the ranks, gaining experience on loan in League One with Oldham Athletic and Sheffield United. Unfortunately, he would later depart Rotherham with just a handful of appearances to his name.

Evans also secured the signatures of Sheffield Wednesday defensive duo Joe Mattock and Lewis Buxton on free transfers. Mattock's capture, in particular, would prove to be a shrewd piece of business. The left-back finished up as the club's second-longest-serving player behind Richard Wood when he left Rotherham for Harrogate Town in May 2022, making over 200 appearances for the club, winning three League One promotions and an EFL Trophy to boot.

Mattock and Buxton were soon joined by former Owls team-mate Chris Maguire, who swapped one South Yorkshire postcode for another on a free transfer, with Evans looking to add to Rotherham's attacking roster. However, the striker, who bagged 18 goals in 79 league games for the Owls, had some amends to make. His celebrations in Wednesday's last-gasp local derby win over Rotherham earlier in the year, when he shushed the home supporters after Atdhe Nuhiu netted the decider in injury time, had touched a nerve. Fortunately for him, it was a game that Millers fans were keen to banish from the memory.

Perhaps the most intriguing new face wasn't such a new face at all, but a familiar one. The return of Emmanuel Ledesma sparked excitement among the fanbase, who were taken aback to see the former Middlesbrough winger return. Supporters had instantly taken to the attacker when he first joined on loan from Boro in November 2014 on an emergency deal. He headed back to the Riverside after making seven appearances in a Millers shirt. Despite Rotherham holding talks with the Teesside club over a potential return – with Evans revealing the club lodged a bid for the player, who ended up being out of their price range – the Argentine was loaned out again to Brighton & Hove Albion until the end of the campaign.

In the summer of 2015, it was confirmed that Ledesma would become a Rotherham player on a permanent basis after the club fought off interest from elsewhere in the Championship. However, things didn't quite go as planned. The 27-year-old started three games – two of which were in the League Cup – and came off the bench a further five times. He was used sparingly for the remainder of a disappointing individual campaign before being released at the end of the season. It was a baffling turn of events that left fans wondering why things didn't quite click the second time around.

The first name on Evans's wishlist was Greg Halford, the utility man released by Nottingham Forest in the summer who had played in the Premier League during his career with a handful of different clubs. Halford had dabbled with positions all over the pitch. Able to play almost anywhere across the backline, he could also do a job in midfield or as a striker if required. Halford, who netted eight goals in 82 appearances for Forest and brought an abundance of Championship experience to the table, was hoping to take his career in a new direction and shake off his utility man tag by homing in on his preferred position up front.

In an interview with the club website, Evans highlighted that Halford was 'quite simply top of that list' he had given to the chairman at the start of pre-season. The player was handed the captain's armband before the campaign got under way, with the Rotherham boss entrusting him with the responsibility of leading the team out in the Championship, but it didn't last long.

'I chose Rotherham over other teams because I was going there as a striker,' Halford recalls. 'That's where I wanted to play. Before, I played at Forest and had a number of games up top for them and scored a lot of goals, so I wanted to rebuild my career as a striker. I wanted to challenge myself.

'I played 45 minutes as a striker in pre-season, then I started the season as a centre-back, where I hadn't trained. I didn't perform on the pitch, which translated to the fans that I wasn't really bothered, and it was tough to win them back over. I was very close to handing in a transfer request after pre-season. At that point, I did regret signing. It was a place I didn't want to work and I didn't have a great first season but, eventually, I got my act together and put it right.'

Another player the Millers were in pursuit of was a 22-year-old winger from Peterborough United. Joe Newell was already acquainted with one of his future comrades at Rotherham, having played alongside Lee Frecklington while coming through the ranks at London Road and all it took was a phone call to the midfielder to get his take on the situation.

'I was lucky in the fact that I knew Lee Frecklington,' Newell explains. 'When I broke through at Peterborough, he was a big help for me coming through. He was one of the older pros that really looked out for me and helped me settle in with the first team.

'I knew he was at Rotherham. The day I drove up to Rotherham for my first day, I rang him and said "Hi, mate. Long time, no speak. Bit of a mad one but I'm coming up to Rotherham now." He was like "Joe, as much as I'd love to see you mate, you need to turn around. This isn't the club for you".

He said, "The way you play football, big Steve isn't going to suit you." Luckily, I didn't listen to him!

'They wanted me to go and train for a week, so I played a trial game first of all against Mainz from Germany in the last pre-season friendly. I was at Peterborough going into the last year of my contract and I told them that I wasn't signing a new deal there. Their policy was that as soon as you're in the last year of your contract, you're on the transfer list, so I knew I was getting sold that summer somehow. Steve Evans, with his connections to Peterborough, and the chairman knew of me.'

Newell was taken on trial by Rotherham during pre-season and eventually, after impressing Evans, put pen to paper on a three-year deal as the Millers parted with an undisclosed fee for the winger. Another astute signing from the Rotherham chief.

Despite his vow not to dip into the loan market as frequently, he turned to Premier League giants Tottenham Hotspur to enquire about taking Grant Ward for a season to give the young midfielder his first taste of Championship football on the back of a short stint at Coventry City in League One the year prior.

'I was at Coventry the season before and Chicago Fire [in Major League Soccer] and I'd done quite well, so there were a few teams interested,' Ward says. 'They asked if I'd be interested and the staff at Spurs heard a few things about Steve Evans, so they told me to go there for a few days first to see how I felt. I went with one of the staff and I liked it.

'It was game time and the opportunity to play in the Championship, which was the highest level I'd played at. I was in League One the season before. Me and the boys at Spurs thought it would be good progression.'

Evans also signed up two central defenders with equally impressive credentials on opposite ends of the spectrum. The Millers snatched up former England youth international and under-17s European champion Tom Thorpe from Manchester United. The 22-year-old, who captained the Red Devils to FA Youth Cup success, boasted a sterling CV but ultimately had a largely forgettable stay at the New York Stadium. On the other hand, Danny Collins had spent the best part of his career plying his trade in the Premier League with the likes of Stoke City and Sunderland, before making the switch to Rotherham from Championship rivals Nottingham Forest.

The goalkeeping department was an entirely different story for the Millers, who, since their promotion back to the Championship, had struggled to find consistency between the sticks. Over the course of the 2014/15 season, Evans had rotated between Wembley shoot-out hero Adam Collin and new signing Scott Loach, before Rotherham made a move to sign Arsenal's Emiliano Martínez. He arrived on a short-term loan deal in March 2015 to cover for injuries as Loach headed out to Yeovil Town.

Future World Cup winner Martínez edged out Collin, putting in an impressive shift to help the Millers to stay up but, once again, Rotherham were on the hunt for a new number one. They turned to Derby County's up-and-coming stopper Kelle Roos. The 23-year-old had caught the Rams' eye while on the books of non-league Nuneaton Town but had only made occasional appearances in cup competitions. Roos would experience his first taste of league football with the Millers. He was handed the number one jersey by Evans, suggesting he would be preferred over Collin. Roos, however, didn't make the best first impression, the keeper shipping ten goals in the opening five games and making several costly errors which led to criticism from supporters. It resulted in his loan spell being cut short just six weeks in.

* * *

If the dramatic fight to the finish in 2014/15 wasn't hair-raising enough, the 2015/16 campaign would hold even more thrills and spills. With just three games of 2014/15 remaining, the Millers looked all but safe for another year until a points deduction sent their season down to the wire.

In April 2015, Rotherham were docked three points and fined £30,000 for fielding an ineligible player in Derby loanee Farrend Rawson. The defender, who arrived on a 28-day youth loan from the Rams in March, was named in the starting line-up for the Millers' home fixture against Brighton in early April. However, the teenager's agreement had expired. The punishment left the club precariously perched one point above the drop zone and right back in the fight against relegation.

'I only played a handful of games and when we played against Brighton my loan was up supposedly, which nobody knew about,' Rawson states. 'I was only 18. I was just playing football and I thought other people would deal with that. We beat Brighton and I woke up on Sunday to find my phone was ringing tenfold. They were asking me to come in and it got released to the media about a points deduction for an ineligible player, which was me, obviously.

'I got sent back to Derby after that, so I didn't have a clue what was going off. Thankfully enough, it didn't affect the season and we managed to stay up because I would've felt devastated massively. As an 18-year-old, I was thinking, "Something must be sorted or I wouldn't be in the team, surely?"'

Nevertheless, Evans's side defied the odds to beat the drop as Millwall, Wigan Athletic and Blackpool were relegated to League One and Rotherham survived their first season back in the Championship after a nine-year absence. However, Rawson faced some backlash.

'I was having people messaging me aggressively and showing a lot of hate towards me,' he continues. 'At one time, people were calling up the club and asking where I lived. I just thought, "This is crazy. How was I supposed to know the loan was up?"'

He put all that behind him when Rotherham came knocking again in the summer to re-sign him on loan, jumping at the chance to return to the New York Stadium and start afresh ahead of the new campaign.

* * *

A host of incomings inevitably meant there would be a few outgoings and it was time to bid a fond farewell to some of the Millers' Wembley heroes. Among those who headed for the exit that summer were Ben Pringle, Craig Morgan and Kári Árnason. The trio had played their part in the club's successive promotions under Evans, writing their names into the history books in the process. However, the team that helped Rotherham to get where they were had slowly been dismantled, player by player.

Pringle departed for second-tier rivals Fulham, having become a popular figure at Rotherham after signing for the club from Derby in the summer of 2011. As free transfers go, Pringle was worth his salt for the club. He was recognised in the PFA's League One team of the year in 2013/14 and his form didn't go unnoticed, either. In the January 2015 transfer window, Millers assistant Paul Raynor told BBC Radio Sheffield that a fee had been agreed with Millwall for the sale of Pringle – who scored 19 goals in 147 league appearances for the club – but the player 'couldn't agree personal terms', feeling it wasn't the 'right move' for him at the time. So, it didn't come as a surprise when he was snapped up by the Cottagers in 2016 on a free transfer.

Skipper Morgan – the club's players' player of the year in 2014/15 – came to an agreement with Wigan. The Welshman, who had earned 23 caps for his country, had been with Rotherham since 2012, when he made the switch from Preston. He was later handed the captaincy by Evans at the beginning of the 2013/14 season after Johnny Mullins departed the club and was at the heart of the defence as the Millers bounced back to the Championship, partnering the outgoing Árnason. During the summer, he revealed that, although he had interest from elsewhere, he wanted to remain a Millers player. However, Morgan later opted to join League One side Wigan, hoping to add another promotion to his CV.

Meanwhile, Árnason, an Icelandic international, swapped the Championship for the Champions League, returning home to the country of his birth, Sweden, to sign for Malmö and it was an opportunity that nobody would begrudge him. Like Morgan, the central defender joined the club in the summer of 2012 as Rotherham geared up for a promotion push. He arrived from Scottish outfit Aberdeen but his experience of playing in the Championship with Plymouth Argyle stood him in good stead when he returned to England. Upon his departure, boss Evans heaped high praise on the 32-year-old, who went on to make his first appearance in a major tournament at Euro 2016, where he found himself coming up against the likes of Cristiano Ronaldo. Evans highlighted Árnason's 'loyalty' to Rotherham when speaking to the club's official website, adding: 'The big fella will always have a place in the hearts of the Millers faithful after playing such a huge part in the success this football club has enjoyed over the last three seasons.'

Now, just three members of the triumphant Wembley squad of 2013/14 remained: Frecklington, Richie Smallwood and Collin. A new team was taking shape under Evans.

'At Rotherham, it's the same every year,' says Smallwood. 'The turnover of players is that huge, it takes some players time to get used to their new team-mates. You see it at most clubs, that bedding-in period. That is a factor each season, certainly while I was there anyway. It's not easy, but you try to hit it off as quickly as possible. The players who got the promotion from League One weren't given a fair chance, but it happens at clubs; they try to move the team on to bring better players in.'

Mark Bradley, Richard Brindley, Rob Milsom, Mat Sadler, Loach and Conor Newton, in addition to academy graduates Tony Thompson and Daniel Rowe, were also informed they would be leaving the club that summer.

Bradley had been with Rotherham since 2010, first signed by Ronnie Moore from Walsall. The defender played 33 times as Rotherham won promotion from League Two in 2012/13. He went on to feature in a further 28 games the following season when the Millers ascended via the play-offs but, after sustaining anterior cruciate ligament damage to his knee in a game against Oldham in March 2014, it would be Bradley's last involvement, later announcing his retirement from professional football.

Fellow full-back Brindley departed after two years. The right-back stepped up following that injury to Bradley but fell out of favour when loan star James Tavernier joined from Newcastle United. After spending time with Colchester United on loan in 2014/15, he made the switch a permanent one.

Milsom joined Rotherham in 2013 after the Millers had won promotion to League One. He played a handful of games in the Championship in 2014/15 but eventually signed for League Two side Notts County. Meanwhile, Sadler transferred to his former club Shrewsbury Town after loans with Crawley Town and Oldham in 2014/15 put him out of the picture. Having been with the Millers for just a year, the full-back failed to make a single appearance during his short stint in South Yorkshire.

Loach would also sign for Notts County, having been unable to make the number one jersey his own since putting pen to paper with the newly promoted Millers in 2014, acting as understudy to Collin in between a series of loan spells with Bury, Peterborough United and Yeovil Town.

Newton joined Cambridge United after his contract at Rotherham expired, making 14 appearances in the Championship after Evans picked the midfielder up from Newcastle. They all made way for a new team to make their mark and consolidate Rotherham's place in the Championship.

* * *

The need to strengthen the backline became even more paramount when, less than a week before players were due to return to training in preparation for the new season, Rotherham received news that defender Kirk Broadfoot had been handed a ten-game ban. The penalty, which ruled him out for a large part of the start of the campaign, was the longest suspension in English football for verbal abuse at the time. Broadfoot's ban surpassed the eight-game penalty issued to Luis Suárez by the FA in 2011 when the then-Liverpool striker was found guilty of racially abusing Manchester United's Patrice Evra.

The incident took place in March 2015 against relegation rivals Wigan. Rotherham suffered a 2-1 defeat in the game when the Millers defender became embroiled in a verbal altercation with James McClean.

A statement from the Football Association stated that Broadfoot would be required pay a fine of £7,500 and complete an education programme as part of his punishment. It read: 'Following an independent regulatory commission hearing, Rotherham United's Kirk Broadfoot will serve an immediate ten-match suspension after a misconduct charge against him was found proven.

'The charge was that during a league fixture between Rotherham and Wigan Athletic on 14 March 2015 Broadfoot used abusive and/or insulting words towards a member of the opposition ... Broadfoot was also fined £7,500 and ordered to complete an education programme.'

Boss Evans faced the prospect of being without one of the previous season's top performers until early October although Broadfoot would surely be raring to go once he'd served his spell on the sidelines.

'I actually finished the end of the season before that really well, so I was feeling really good. I'd done a lot of fitness work with Warney [Paul Warne],' Broadfoot says. 'Me and him were doing a lot of extra training, so I was ready to go, but I couldn't. The amount of running we did during that time, I felt really fit when I was ready to go. The thing about being in England is there are so many games. It [the duration of the suspension] wasn't as long as if I was up in Scotland; you were looking at maybe four months to get ten games in up there.'

* * *

As was tradition, Rotherham kicked off pre-season with their annual friendly fixture against local non-league outfit Parkgate, giving fans the chance to run the rule over a host of new faces. Steve Evans fielded two different teams either side of the break. Ledesma, Paul Green, Grant Ward, Danny Ward and Jerry Yates all made the scoresheet in an emphatic display as the Millers got the campaign under way with a 6-0 victory.

Pre-season continued with trips to semi-professional sides Stocksbridge Park Steels and Alfreton Town. Smallwood, Grant Ward and Jonson Clarke-Harris were all on target in a 3-0 win at Stocksbridge before the Millers slipped to a 3-2 defeat to Alfreton, with Ward grabbing both goals. Nonetheless, it provided a good workout for the side before they headed north of the border to Scotland for a tour of Evans's homeland.

On their travels, Rotherham picked up a 3-0 win against Greenock Morton – Halford, Frecklington and Clarke-Harris the scorers – and a 1-0 triumph over Dundee, courtesy of a Green strike, before playing out a 1-1 draw with Partick Thistle in which Matt Derbyshire opened his account for pre-season.

In the penultimate fixture in the pre-season schedule, Rotherham hosted Leicester City who, unbeknown to the crowd of just over 3,600 inside the stadium that evening, would go on to be crowned Premier League champions that season. Riyad Mahrez and David Nugent struck in the second half for the Foxes to give them a 2-0 lead before Grant Ward halved the deficit with ten minutes remaining.

Rotherham went out on a high when they entertained Bundesliga outfit Mainz in South Yorkshire a week before the season got under way. This time, it was Derbyshire and Jordan Bowery among the goals for the Millers in a 2-1 victory. That meant that Evans's men finished pre-season with five wins in eight. All the signs suggested Rotherham fans could hold high hopes for the new campaign. However, nobody could have predicted what was in store and one of the Millers' new recruits, Mattock, summed it up perfectly when reflecting on his time at the club.

'The previous three years before, when I was at Sheffield Wednesday, was all pretty much middle of the table – not really threatening for the play-offs but not really at risk of going down. It was mainly a steady Championship season,' he says. 'Going into Rotherham, straight from the off, we were on the back foot. It was almost like "Welcome to Rotherham. Here we go."'

Chapter Two
Slow Start

AT A glance, the Championship would be a tough beast to tackle, as it is every year for 'teams like Rotherham' (what has become the Millers fanbase's favourite self-deprecating tagline). It is a division widely considered to be the most competitive league in England and some might go as far as saying the most entertaining second tier in the world. So much so that even the likes of Pep Guardiola and Jürgen Klopp have attested to the quality of the English football pyramid and confessed to indulging themselves in a game from the lower tiers from time to time. With the Championship comes the thrill of the chase at both ends of the table, although Rotherham United fans almost certainly knew where they stood.

The 2014/15 season saw Hull City, Burnley and Queens Park Rangers all relegated from the Premier League and rejoining the Championship ahead of 2015/16. The Tigers, who had been playing in the Europa League the season prior, fell through the top-flight trapdoor after a two-year stay. Meanwhile, it was a flying visit to the Premier League for Burnley and QPR, with both clubs having won promotion from the Championship in 2013/14 before being relegated after a single season.

Coming up from League One, Bristol City were crowned champions in 2014/15, with Milton Keynes Dons joining them as runners-up after clinching the remaining automatic promotion spot. Preston North End, beaten by Rotherham United in the play-off semi-finals in 2013/14, finally made it to Wembley the following year where they vanquished Swindon Town 4-0 under the arch to complete the Championship line-up for the new season.

For want of a better cliché, the Millers were well aware they were something of a small fish in a big pond, in the same way they'd been the underdogs in their maiden season back in the Championship. You only had to look at the odds being offered by the bookmakers to see that it was a foregone conclusion that Rotherham would succumb to the drop after just about managing to stay up in 2014/15.

The strength of the division was only accentuated by the fact that the two teams Rotherham won promotion alongside in 2013/14 – Wolverhampton Wanderers and Brentford – hadn't taken long to settle into life in the Championship, with both clubs already competing at the top end of the table. In 2014/15, the Bees finished in fifth but failed to beat Middlesbrough in the play-off semi-finals, whilst Wolves narrowly missed out on a top-six finish on goal difference. And it wasn't too long before both were Premier League clubs.

Fixture release day was pencilled in for Wednesday, 17 June. It was the day when Rotherham would find out when and where their Championship campaign would get under way. As it transpired, the Millers would get the season started on home soil at the New York Stadium. Newly promoted MK Dons were the first visitors to South Yorkshire, with Karl Robinson's team about to embark on their inaugural season in the second tier. Rotherham were looking for their first-ever victory over the Buckinghamshire club. Since the two sides first met in October 2005, the Millers were without a win in their six previous encounters with MK Dons, which was perhaps the first bad omen.

The last time the club had won their opening fixture in the second tier was in August 2002 when Rotherham romped to a 6-0 victory over Millwall. There were parallels to be drawn between former Millers manager Ronnie Moore's team and Steve Evans's side. Back in the Championship for the first time since 1983, Rotherham had clung on to their second-tier status by the skin of their teeth in 2001/02 while Millwall had made it to the play-off semi-finals. For that reason, it was a shock to everyone when striker Darren Byfield put four past the Lions at The Den in the 2002/03 curtain raiser.

The 2015/16 campaign also marked the first time Rotherham would kick off their league campaign on home soil since the 2012/13 season. The Millers hosted Burton Albion in August 2012 at the newly built New York Stadium, which opened its doors to the town and welcomed its football club home for their first competitive fixture. Evans's side ran out 3-0 winners over the Brewers in League Two and it was a game which paved the way back to the Championship. Nobody could deny that there had certainly been some good days at the office for Rotherham on their own patch in recent years, but this wasn't about to be one of them.

Saturday, 8 August 2015
New York Stadium
EFL Championship
Rotherham United 1 (Derbyshire 13')
MK Dons 4 (Hall 5', Collins OG 28', Bowditch 35', Baker 75')
Nobody was as clued up on the temperament of Millers manager Evans as the Rotherham supporters themselves. In the three-and-a-bit years that he had been at the club, the Scot and his assistant Paul Raynor were renowned for cutting an animated duo on the touchline – whether in an expression of euphoria or anger. It depended on the outcome on the pitch. Every manager has their own philosophy and style of man-

management; some prefer the subtle arm around the shoulder approach whereas others believe players need to be hit with the home truths. However he did it, Evans had got the best out of his players. Two promotions and a season of survival did the talking on that front. He wasn't afraid to speak his mind, but that was all part of the ethos that made up the fabric of Rotherham United; fans of the club appreciated having somebody to speak up on their behalf and fight the fight when called upon.

Evans didn't shy away from giving his players an earful when the occasion called for a dressing-down and if there was ever a display that warranted it, it could well have been watching his squad go down to a 4-1 defeat at the hands of MK Dons. On the contrary, Evans insisted in his post-match press conference that it was a 'lesson learned' and there was 'no shouting and bawling in the dressing room' in the wake of the result, although he asserted that Rotherham would have to take the result 'bang in the face'. However, it was a game that suggested the club were in for a tough ride.

If Evans's side thought they might be eased into the season with a clash against the division's newbies, they couldn't have been more wrong. The Dons made a dream start to life in the Championship. Instead, it was the Millers who looked wet behind the ears.

The boss named eight debutants in the starting line-up, with Kelle Roos selected between the sticks while Greg Halford, Tom Thorpe and Danny Collins formed the defensive line and Chris Maguire, Grant Ward and Aidy White each made their bows. Richie Smallwood, Danny Ward and Matt Derbyshire were the only players to keep their places from the team that played out a goalless draw with Leeds United on the final day of the 2014/15 season.

Rotherham got off on the wrong foot inside five minutes when a calamity at the back allowed Rob Hall to tap home from close range and put MK Dons ahead. However, the hosts regrouped and less than ten minutes later, they were back on level terms. Maguire won the Millers a corner which he delivered into the box for Derbyshire to score with a glancing header, the club's leading scorer from the 2014/15 season getting off the mark on the opening day. The striker wheeled away in delight, leaping into the air in celebration.

But with just under half an hour played, Rotherham fell behind again. Jordan Spence's cross caught out Roos at his near post. Things went from bad to worse when Dean Bowditch took his opportunity to make it 3-1. Evans tried to switch things up at the break, with experienced midfield duo Lee Frecklington and Paul Green coming on for Grant Ward and White, but the changes were to no avail. By the 75th minute, MK Dons were 4-1 up and cruising courtesy of substitute Carl Baker.

By the end of the season, the fixture would prove to be a crucial match-up in the battle for survival, but there was plenty of football to be played between now and then.

Tuesday, 11 August 2015
New York Stadium
League Cup
Rotherham United 1 (Bowery 45')
Cambridge United 0

Evans's men had the chance to bounce back in another competition as Rotherham's short-lived run in the League Cup – under the guise of the Capital One Cup – began at home to League Two outfit Cambridge United. Unlike the Millers, the U's had been encouraged by their start to the campaign, beating Newport County 3-0 in their opening fixture. After their reality check against MK Dons, the Millers were eager to put that result behind them and pick up a first victory of the campaign, albeit in the cup.

Rotherham have history in the competition, having made it to the inaugural final in 1961. They faced Aston Villa in a two-legged affair and, after beating the Villans 2-0 in the home tie at Millmoor, the South Yorkshire team were in pole position to go all the way and become the first team to lift the League Cup. Up until the final half hour at Villa Park, Rotherham – managed by another Scotsman, Tom Johnston – were in the driving seat. Two goals in quick succession drew Joe Mercer's Villa level and the First Division side went on to win it in extra time.

Under Evans, the club returned to the scene of that heartbreak in August 2013 when they drew Villa away in the second round of the tournament. The Rotherham boss was usually up for the cup, admitting that he'd have started himself against the West Midlands team – who Rotherham lost 3-0 to on the day – had his fitness levels been up to scratch. However, he'd have been getting carried away if he said he was thinking beyond the upcoming clash with Cambridge at that point in time.

The Millers boss fielded a strong side for the first-round tie against Cambridge, with the likes of Lewis Buxton, Emmanuel Ledesma and Jordan Bowery given the chance to stretch their legs and stake a claim for Rotherham's next league game away at Nottingham Forest.

Just before the end of the first half, it was Bowery who scored what would be the only goal of the game and his last in a Millers shirt, heading in Joe Newell's cross. Bowery had become the club's record signing in June 2014 and scored five in his first year in South Yorkshire before being linked with a move away from the club the following summer. The former Aston Villa striker headed out on loan to Bradford City in November before Rotherham cancelled his contract to allow him to join Oxford United on a permanent deal in January, with then-manager Neil Redfearn declaring Bowery had no future at the club.

A narrow victory was enough to see the Millers book their place in the second round of the competition. The question now was whether they could dust themselves off and go again against Championship opposition.

Saturday, 15 August 2015
City Ground
EFL Championship
Nottingham Forest 2 (Mills 45', Antonio 61')
Rotherham United 1 (Collins 13')

Rotherham didn't need reminding that slow and steady rarely wins the race in the Championship. It's no great revelation that when the Millers stayed up in 2022/23 under the joint tutelage of Paul Warne and Matt Taylor, they enjoyed their best-ever start to a season in the Championship.

However, in 2015/16, they were already at risk of getting left behind and an opening day defeat to MK Dons might well have sent out a message to rival clubs that the Millers were there for the taking. For the first time since a 2-0 win over Huddersfield Town in March – one of just three triumphs away from home in 2014/15, having also beaten Millwall and Wigan Athletic – Rotherham were looking for victory on their travels when they played Nottingham Forest in their first away game of the season.

There were a handful of former Forest men in the Millers side. Collins, Halford and Derbyshire were among those ex-Reds. Rotherham fans also got to see Joe Mattock make his debut after returning from injury, with the former Sheffield Wednesday defender selected as Evans's first-choice left-back. And it was Collins who headed Rotherham into the lead against his ex-employers from a Newell corner.

'It helps going into a new club and starting well,' Newell states. 'The year before, I'd won player of the year awards at Peterborough. I was at a good age and really motivated to go and do well. Even though the team was struggling, I got five or six assists in the first couple of months. All the goals and all but one of my assists were before January.

'Steve Evans believed in me and gave me a lot of confidence. He chucked me in there and said "Go and play your stuff." The first half of the season was really good for me. For a team in the relegation zone, it was a good return.'

However, on the stroke of half-time, Matt Mills's header looped over Roos and into the back of the net to cancel out Collins's opener and Forest turned it around in the second half when Michail Antonio couldn't miss to make it 2-1.

Evans was surprisingly upbeat after the game, insisting post-match: 'If we play like that in the Championship for the rest of the season, we will come away with a lot of points.' Others needed some convincing, but one thing Millers fans – who travelled in their numbers to the City Ground, with over 1,500 away supporters in attendance – were certain about was that it was going to be a long season.

Tuesday, 18 August 2015
New York Stadium
EFL Championship
Rotherham United 0
Preston North End 0

The eager anticipation of the new season was quickly starting to wear off as pragmatism set in. Fortunately for the Millers, there wasn't quite as much riding on their home clash with Preston North End compared to the last time the two teams met 15 months earlier. In May 2014, North End made the trip across the Pennines in a battle of the roses when Rotherham ran out 3-1 winners on the night at the New York Stadium to book their place in the 2013/14 League One play-off final.

After playing out a 1-1 draw at Deepdale in the first leg of the semi-final, when Alex Revell and Joe Garner found the back of their net for their respective teams, the Millers had to come from behind on their own territory. Paul Gallagher opened the scoring for Preston before goals from Wes Thomas, Frecklington and Kieran Agard took Rotherham to Wembley, where they would go on to beat Leyton Orient to win promotion. Now, Preston were back in the Championship after following in the Millers' footsteps the previous season and winning promotion at Wembley.

After being left out of the matchday squad for the first three games of the season, it looked as though Jonson Clarke-Harris's time in South Yorkshire may be up. The striker, who surpassed Bowery as the club's most expensive player when he joined the Millers for an undisclosed fee from Oldham Athletic in September 2014, had scored three goals in 16 appearances for Rotherham in 2014/15 before heading out on loan to League One sides MK Dons and Doncaster Rovers.

'I'd only just got my foot in the door in the Championship at that stage of my career,' explains Clarke-Harris. 'There were a lot of good players – and a lot of good strikers – at the club at the same time who I looked up to. I knew they were going to be ahead of me in the team at the time. They were older and more experienced and just overall better players at the time. It was mostly about minutes for me – as many minutes as I could possibly play.

'It was Danny Ward at the time who picked up a bit of a calf injury and I was always going into the boss saying, "Give me a chance, give me a chance." For about seven or eight games, I had a run and came out with about three goals in that time and then Danny Ward was back fit again. It was one of those where it was tough to stay in the team because you can see what Danny Ward has gone on to do in his career.'

After being linked with another spell away from the New York Stadium, Evans eventually called upon Clarke-

Harris for the visit of Preston. The 21-year-old was among the substitutes as he was handed a second chance, but manager Evans had issued him a warning.

'I like Jonson Clarke-Harris as a player, but I have just reminded him that if he drops it, he's out,' Evans said at the time. 'Playing like that, he is a top player in the Championship, but he has to come in and work hard and be committed and he knows that now. We're covering old ground here, since we had a chat ten days ago where he came in the office and had a cup of tea and a digestive. He made it clear that we were going to see a Jonson Clarke-Harris that wanted to earn the right to be here because he was on his way out.'

'To be fair, we had more than one conversation!' the striker adds. 'I was young, I was naïve and I thought I should be playing every game but other players were performing better than me in training and on a Saturday as well.

'I probably was too patient and I probably should've knocked on his door and said, "Why am I not starting? Why am I not playing?" because at the start of pre-season the next year, I ended up getting injured and that was it, my time at Rotherham was pretty much done from there.

'The club got me when I was young and it could have gone one way or the other. It went the way where I got injured and I had to go out and get minutes. I can say my first stint at Rotherham didn't work out the way I wanted it to or the way the club wanted it to. Unfortunately, that was the sad way it had to end.'

Rotherham picked up their first point of the season after the game finished goalless. It got Evans's side off and running with a first clean sheet in the league, too, making Bristol City – who would also become embroiled in a relegation battle for large parts of the season – the only team yet to get off the mark for 2015/16. There were chances for both teams, but the Lilywhites' perfect defensive record prevailed, with the

Millers unable to find a way past their new loan keeper, future England number one Jordan Pickford.

League table:

Position	*Club*	*Pl*	*GD*	*Pts*
20	Reading	2	-1	1
21	Queens Park Rangers	2	-2	1
22	Rotherham United	3	-4	1
23	Bolton Wanderers	3	-4	1
24	Bristol City	2	-4	0

Saturday, 22 August 2015
Loftus Road
EFL Championship
Queens Park Rangers 4 (Chery 42', 50', Austin 63', 90')
Rotherham United 2 (Clarke-Harris 72', Thorpe 88')
Old habits die hard and Rotherham found that out the hard way later in the week when they travelled to Queens Park Rangers.

They held on until just before half-time when Dutchman Tjaronn Chery scored the first of his two goals. Five minutes into the second period, the Millers were exposed once again as Chery doubled QPR's advantage. Charlie Austin grabbed a goal with just over an hour played as the in-demand striker, who scored 18 goals for the club in the Premier League the season prior, made it 3-0 and it appeared to be game over.

Clarke-Harris repaid Evans's faith in handing the striker a recall to the starting line-up when he curled in an effort from outside the area to reduce the arrears with 72 minutes played but Rotherham still trailed 3-1.

'I cut in on the inside from the right and there was a little chip over the defenders, and I've bent it into the far corner. I do believe the keeper should have saved it to be fair, but I'll take it!' Clarke-Harris says. 'When it's going against you, it's going against you. It's how do you break that cycle of constantly losing games? I just felt like we needed a bit of luck on our side and we didn't seem to get it.

'You can't shine unless everybody else is shining as well. I've always said this throughout my whole career. I'm only as good as the players around me and this isn't me saying the players around me were not to my calibre, because these players were better than me at the time.

'The way that we played in the Championship back then is the typical Steve Evans way but football has changed now. A lot of teams were playing football, whereas we were going high press, high attack, 100 per cent and 100mph, entertaining the fans of Rotherham. Even if we went down or we stayed up, as long as it was entertaining for the fans, that was all the chairman and the boss could really ask for. It would be nice to be finishing 14th to tenth or in the top half of the table, but at that point of the club being in the Championship, we just weren't there.'

Thorpe was on hand for a simple tap-in at the back post and there was hope that the Millers could salvage a point with the scoreline poised at 3-2. However, when Maguire tripped Sebastian Polter inside the box, Austin bagged a brace when he converted from the penalty spot and sealed a 4-2 victory for QPR.

It was glaringly obvious that Rotherham needed to tighten up at the back and that they were still missing defender Kirk Broadfoot's presence on the pitch. Former Millers manager and fitness coach at the time Paul Warne once jokingly labelled the defender, who joined Rotherham from Blackpool in the summer of 2014, as one of footballer's biggest moaners.

'I moaned a lot because I wanted the best for everybody,' Broadfoot explains. 'Yeah, I moaned at everybody if they did something wrong but that was just setting standards and demands of people, but I'd always encourage people if they did something well. I just wanted things doing right, whether it was on or off the training pitch. I was trying to push the club forward. I'm one of those personalities that will say, "That's not good enough."

'I wasn't able to play at the time, so I couldn't moan at the players. I think that got the best out of the players because they'd say, "We miss you when you're not playing because we're not on edge." Whereas if I was playing, I'd be on their back making sure they were doing their job. Joe Newell always said to me, "It's better when you play because you keep me on edge if I switch off." I was doing it for the team's sake, not to be this horrible personality or bad guy. It's easier when you're sitting in the stand because you see it a lot clearer than when you're down on the pitch.'

'He was a great guy, Broady – a real funny bloke,' Newell concurs. 'If I was having a lazy day or didn't start well in a game, he'd be foaming at the mouth and calling you all the names under the sun. That's what I needed as a young lad at that age. You need the older lads in the team to show you what's on the line and what's at stake and show you how it should be done.'

Tuesday, 25 August 2015
New York Stadium
League Cup
Rotherham United 1 (Green 80')
Norwich City 2 (Howson 22', Van Wolfswinkel 68')
When the so-called big hitters enter the hat in round three – the likes of Manchester United, Manchester City, Liverpool, Arsenal and Tottenham Hotspur – it's only natural that you might hold on to some hope of making it through round two, if only to have a big day out at Old Trafford or the Emirates, for instance.

Rotherham fans had witnessed some classics in the League Cup in years gone by. In 2003/04, after overcoming Colchester United in the second round of the competition in front of a crowd of just over 2,000, a date at Highbury was their reward. The Millers faced Arsenal in the third round in front of over 27,000 supporters. It also happened to be the day that a young Cesc Fàbregas made his debut for the Gunners. Rotherham's Darren Byfield headed in a 90th-minute equaliser before keeper Mike Pollitt was sent off in extra time and Arsenal went on to win 9-8 on penalties.

However, the 2008/09 season was the last time Rotherham had made it past the second round of the competition – making it to the fourth round, where they lost to Stoke City – and there would be no such cup run seven years on.

At least it provided a welcome distraction from their poor league form when the Millers drew newly promoted Premier League side Norwich City at home. Rotherham old boy Lewis Grabban – the club's top scorer in 2011/12 in League Two who was poached by Bournemouth for a six-figure fee – caused a stir when he was said to have fled Norwich's team hotel before kick-off after being named on the bench. It was reported that the striker was unhappy with being left out of the starting line-up amid interest from the Cherries, who were circling to re-sign Grabban, only for Norwich to reject their advances.

Grabban, who was absent from the game, was eventually suspended and fined by the Canaries.

Rotherham put up a fight but goals from Jonny Howson and Norwich's club record signing Ricky van Wolfswinkel saw the Millers ousted from the competition despite a consolation goal from Green and their focus returned to the Championship and getting their season back on track.

Saturday, 29 August 2015
New York Stadium
EFL Championship
Rotherham United 1 (Clarke-Harris 72')
Fulham 3 (Pringle 7', McCormack 16', Woodrow 90+3')
A man who was so used to rippling the net at the New York Stadium to the cheers from the home supporters came back to haunt his ex-employers with his new club Fulham as a challenging month drew to a disappointing close. And it took Ben Pringle just seven minutes to rediscover that familiar feeling.

'It's always strange when you come up against your former team-mates, especially the ones who you've been in an amazing dressing room with,' keeper Adam Collin notes. 'It's good to see them kicking on as well and moving on in their careers. Fulham had a very strong team that day.'

The Millers were staring down the barrel at a third straight defeat in all competitions and a fourth loss in five league games, while the west Londoners were eyeing a first Championship win of the season. Despite being unable to stop Rotherham bowing out of the League Cup against Norwich, Collin retained his place between the sticks, with Roos only on the bench after a string of poor performances in the league. He would soon return to his parent club Derby County when Rotherham opted to terminate his loan agreement.

Collin recalls: 'It's one of the highest levels I've managed to play in my career. I managed the step up really well and played at Championship level to help that team stay up in the first season which was a huge achievement for me personally and the club. I really enjoyed going to some different grounds and some big football clubs.

'You get some huge clubs and some world-class players in there now. Emi Martínez has gone on to achieve huge things in the game and he's one of the best goalkeepers in the world now. When he won the World Cup, I wasn't too disappointed that he came in to take my place!'

Collin was unable to deal with Moussa Dembélé's header early in the contest and it had to be Pringle who was ready and waiting to make it 1-0 to the visitors. Fulham doubled their advantage from the penalty spot with 16 minutes played as Ross McCormack stepped up and converted.

In the second half, Rotherham were awarded a penalty of their own when referee Geoff Eltringham handed the Millers a chance to get back into the game. Jazz Richards knocked Green off his feet and Derbyshire took up his position from 12 yards. However, Fulham stopper Andy Lonergan made the save.

Rotherham did get one back through Clarke-Harris. The striker took on the Cottagers' defence and picked his spot from outside the box with a well-taken goal. It was clear that Rotherham would have to settle for just the one point from their opening five league games once Cauley Woodrow put the game beyond doubt in added time.

Evans admitted he wouldn't have been happy with the performance if he was a Rotherham fan watching from the stands. His side were bottom of the pile five games into the season. Something needed to change and quickly. Nevertheless, there was bound to be a gulf between the Millers and the teams they were coming up against. In comparison to Rotherham's £4.8m spent on wages the previous year, the Cottagers had splashed out £60.4m. It was always going to be an arduous ask.

Meanwhile, a situation unfolding away from the pitch was the matter of the club captaincy. Less than a week after losing to Fulham, it was confirmed that Evans had stripped Halford of the role, with Frecklington replacing him. Since making the switch from Forest in the summer, the 30-year-old had skippered the side in the opening seven games, which resulted in five defeats, and the Millers manager explained that taking away the armband would see Halford 'freed from the extra burden of responsibility'. It appeared that everything that could go wrong was doing so for Rotherham.

'Over the last week or so, I have had to make some tough decisions,' Evans told the club's official website. 'After meeting with the chairman, he has asked me to do what it takes to continue to move the club forward in the short and long term and, as a result, several changes have been implemented.

'With the benefit of hindsight, I have to accept I made the wrong decision with the captaincy at the start of the season, but I firmly believe that the changes we have made today will benefit players individually and the squad as a whole.

'I have never been afraid to make a decision or to indeed recognise when I have got something wrong. When I do, I take action. The opposite is to be stubborn and do nothing about it. That will never be something I am guilty of.'

Frecklington recalls: 'I was disappointed because it's not nice to change halfway through the season and I felt for Greg, but he was amazing with me through it. To be given it was a huge honour and something I really relished. I was the sort of player that always cared, so I felt a lot of responsibility was on me because I'd been at the club for a few years and there weren't many of us still left. I felt like a big part of the club and what it was about. I felt I had to lead by example.'

The midfielder – who made the permanent switch to Rotherham in January 2013 after a successful loan spell from Peterborough United – had been a cornerstone of the team since his arrival, scoring one of the most memorable goals in the club's history when he found the back of the net on the final day of the 2012/13 season against Aldershot to promote Rotherham and effectively relegate the Shots. Now, he had the added responsibility of the armband and everyone was right behind him.

Saturday, 12 September 2015
The Valley
EFL Championship
Charlton Athletic 1 (Bauer 65')
Rotherham United 1 (Rawson 38')

There were question marks over Evans's future as the manager of Rotherham, with League One side Peterborough United circling. It was no coincidence that Peterborough was the place the Millers boss – whose wife and children were born in the city, while several of his in-laws followed the Posh – had called home for 20 years at the time. Naturally, there was an attraction there for Evans, who had been linked to the position vacated by Darren Ferguson at London Road at the end of 2014/15. He dispelled those initial rumours, saying that Peterborough was the 'right club at the wrong time' and insisted that he would remain at the New York Stadium after Rotherham confirmed their second-tier status for the 2015/16 season.

Fast forward to September 2015 and it only added fuel to the fire when his assistant Raynor was sent to stand in for the manager on press duties ahead of Rotherham's trip to south London to take on Charlton Athletic. After playing out a 1-1 draw with the Addicks, Evans insisted that he hadn't been distracted by talk of Peterborough's interest and his focus had been solely on his current employer's two upcoming league games against Charlton and Brighton. In the end, Posh chairman Darragh MacAnthony took to social media to confirm he had ruled out a move for the Rotherham manager. Graham Westley would go on to get the job, but Evans eventually got the opportunity to fulfil his ambition of managing Peterborough later down the line in 2018.

For now, he had enough on his plate and his own problems to deal with. With Roos sent back to Derby, Rotherham were in the market for a new stopper to not only keep Collin on his toes but to fix the small matter of the club being in possession of the division's worst defensive record. The Millers had conceded 13 goals in their first five league games and it would be their downfall if they didn't act fast.

Lee Camp was the answer, as it turned out. An experienced goalkeeper who had been released by newly promoted Bournemouth, he had played for a number of clubs and Rotherham and Evans knew what Camp was about. The 31-year-old had faced the South Yorkshire side three times in the previous season for the Cherries – twice in the Championship and once in the FA Cup. He managed a clean sheet in Bournemouth's 2-0 win over Rotherham at the New York Stadium just a fortnight after Eddie Howe's side knocked the Millers out of the FA Cup in a 5-1 win.

He was – and still is – a player synonymous with the Championship, previously holding the record for the most appearances in the second tier by the time he finished up, playing over 500 games for the likes of Derby County, Norwich, QPR, Forest, Bournemouth and later Sunderland and Birmingham City.

The former England under-21 international didn't need an introduction to some of his new team-mates, either. Camp had played with Derbyshire in the Three Lions' youth set-up when the pair were called up to represent their country in the first-ever game at the new Wembley. The fixture against Italy ended in a 3-3 draw, with Derbyshire grabbing a goal for England.

'I'm by no means a perfect goalkeeper but I always tend to be pretty consistent in my work and pretty reliable,' Camp says. 'Even as a young lad, I was always told I'd never achieve what I wanted to achieve and I was always faced with elements of negativity and criticism.

'When I came into the football club, there'd been a bit of inconsistency with goalkeepers and loan goalkeepers. That was the one thing that Steve Evans wanted to achieve, to bring somebody in as their goalkeeper who could play regularly and they didn't have to worry about. I was looking for an opportunity coming out of Bournemouth to get back playing. I think it went hand-in-hand and it ticked boxes on both sides.'

After being involved in a promotion push with Bournemouth, he was under no illusions that this season he would be battling at the other end of the table to keep the Millers up. And he soon had supporters comparing him to one of the club's goalkeeping greats, Mike Pollitt. Pollitt, who returned to Rotherham later down the line in his career as a keeper coach, set a new club record for the most clean sheets kept by a Millers gloveman. That milestone was crucial to Rotherham's fight against relegation in his second spell with the club between 2001 and 2005 when they managed four consecutive seasons competing in the second tier. The former Wigan Athletic man eventually got his big move to the Premier League. Although a dependable stopper is hard to come by when you're on a budget, Rotherham have managed to unearth a few gems over the years, even as recently as Swedish international Viktor Johansson or 'the Viking' as he became affectionately known. A figure who could be trusted between the sticks has often been the difference between success and failure.

'Expectation grew at Rotherham very quickly,' Camp continues. 'Being down the leagues and having no stadium, then the new owner comes in and builds a fantastic stadium and they have back-to-back promotions and success at Wembley. It raises expectations. The natural progression after one year in the Championship is to look to become more established. It was a tough start to the year and those expectations weren't fulfilled. It's a working town and in most clubs up in the north, if you aren't doing a shift, you get told. Everybody at the football club knew that the progression was there but knowing it and achieving it are two different things.'

Evans also strengthened in other areas with the additions of Norwich City duo Tony Andreu and Vadis Odjidja-Ofoe, having taken a liking to the pair in the Canaries' League Cup win over his team in August. Andreu joined the club until January while Odjidja-Ofoe signed a one-month emergency loan.

All three of the new recruits were handed their full debuts when Rotherham returned to action against Charlton following September's international break. It was a first point on the road for Evans's side, who drew 1-1 with the Addicks.

Defender Farrend Rawson scored his first goal for Rotherham just before half-time in what was a slightly controversial moment in the game. Clarke-Harris's free kick took a deflection to carry it behind and referee Keith Stroud awarded a corner. However, Charlton felt it should have been a goal kick, with the ball appearing to come off Millers skipper Frecklington. From Newell's resulting set piece, Rawson found himself unmarked at the far post, tapping home to make it 1-0, much to the indignation of the home crowd. Meanwhile, Grant Ward was substituted at the break and wouldn't appear again until playing the final ten minutes of a 2-0 win over Birmingham City just under a month later.

'In pre-season, everything was quite relaxed,' Ward says. 'The season started, we played MK Dons in the first game and I was playing in midfield. We were losing 3-1 at half-time and I got subbed and I wasn't in the squad for the next two or three games. We had two games – one was in London at Charlton and the next one was in Brighton, so we stayed down – and I wasn't in the squad for both games. There were a few of us not in the squad, so we were running around London with a GPS on. That wasn't the best time and the team was struggling as well. It just wasn't clicking.

'At the start, there were contrasting styles. For myself, I'd come from Spurs and I was at Coventry where they play good football and it's all on the floor. Steve [Evans] was a bit more direct in his style of play. To start with, it was a culture shock and I didn't adapt to it straight away. I'd be trying to get the ball short off the defenders and they'd be playing it long and as the ball drops down in the middle of the park, I'm not going to get the second ball.

'It takes a few games to get used to the pace of it. You've got some big teams in there coming down from the Premier League. If you make mistakes in that league, as we did at the start, you get punished.'

Stopper Nick Pope kept the Addicks in the game before Patrick Bauer levelled for the home team. Simon Makienok put it on a plate for Bauer to produce a simple finish and make it 1-1 with 65 minutes on the clock. The performance was better from Rotherham, but they remained rooted to the bottom of the table, with just two points on the board and league leaders Brighton & Hove Albion up next.

Tuesday, 15 September 2015
American Express Stadium
EFL Championship
Brighton & Hove Albion 2 (Hemed 27', Stephens 67')
Rotherham United 1 (Clarke-Harris 71')
Rotherham were now without a league win since April, when they had beaten Reading 2-1 at the New York Stadium to seal their Championship survival. It always felt unlikely that it would come when Rotherham made a midweek trip to table-toppers Brighton, who had maintained a 100 per cent record at the Amex and were eyeing a fourth league victory on the bounce. The Seagulls duly extended their lead on closest rivals Middlesbrough to five points while Evans's side were made to wait for that all-important first win.

'It's really difficult losing games of football on a regular basis,' Frecklington reflects. 'We had quite a lot of new players come in at that time as well, which makes it tricky. We were disappointed because we'd had three successful years where we were used to winning and having a great atmosphere around the camp but to then start losing games, you could see it was starting to get difficult.

'It was everything you can imagine; a lack of confidence, unhappiness around the training group and lack of belief. When you lose games, it becomes a habit. You go into games thinking "Oh no, we're not going to win." Then it carries on and carries on.'

Watched by a crowd of over 21,000 supporters – a hardened proportion of which had made the long trip down from South Yorkshire – Brighton wrapped up a 2-1 win. Inside half an hour, after missing a handful of chances to take the lead, Tomer Hemed made it 1-0 to the Seagulls in the 27th minute. Chris Hughton's side struck again in the second half. Blue-and-white-striped shirts were lining up to find a way through before it dropped to Dale Stephens and Rotherham's hopes of getting back into the game dwindled away. They pulled a goal back when Clarke-Harris made it 2-1 with 71 minutes gone. The striker headed in Newell's free kick, but it was too little, too late. Despite the outcome, Evans was resolute in his stance, sending a message to Millers fans.

'My job at Rotherham United is far from finished,' he said, affirming that as long as chairman Tony Stewart wanted him at the club, that was where he would remain.

League table:

Position	*Club*	*Pl*	*GD*	*Pts*
20	Huddersfield Town	7	-4	6
21	Brentford	6	-3	5
22	Bristol City	7	-6	5
23	Blackburn Rovers	6	-3	3
24	Rotherham United	7	-9	2

Chapter Three

Fond Farewell

A FIRST win of the season eventually came against Cardiff City at a sun-kissed New York Stadium. But just as the tide started to turn for Rotherham United, nobody anticipated it would be Steve Evans's swansong in South Yorkshire. For the first time since their return to the second tier, Rotherham registered back-to-back victories – against Cardiff and Birmingham City – but just two days after that result at St Andrew's, the club parted company with Evans after three-and-a-half years in charge. It came as a shock, to say the least.

A 2-0 win over Birmingham helped the Millers to claw their way out of the bottom three and jump up four places to 20th position, which was where Evans and his assistant Paul Raynor left them. They could hold their heads high at the job they'd done. They'd left the club in a much better place than they'd found it – that much was certain.

When the Scot was first named as the new Rotherham manager in April 2012, it was easy to see why chairman Tony Stewart had identified Evans as the man to spearhead a promotion push from League Two. Evans and Raynor, who had been in charge at Crawley Town since 2007 prior to joining Rotherham, oversaw a record-breaking campaign in which Crawley stormed to the Conference title in 2010/11 with 105 points on the board. The duo helped the club to make it consecutive promotions in Crawley's inaugural Football League campaign. However, they quit the West Sussex team, who were on the brink of promotion to the third tier in April 2012, as Evans passed up a season in League One to drop back down to League Two with Rotherham.

For any prospective manager stepping foot inside the club at the time, they might have had to use their imagination to envision what could be on the back of a tumultuous few years for the Millers, but Evans – who also had experience managing in the Football League with Boston United – saw the potential. After his first promotion at Rotherham in 2012/13, he said as much, explaining that he left Crawley for a club he believed he could take all the way to the Championship. He took a gamble and it was one that paid off.

As for Evans himself, he came through the ranks as a player with Bolton Wanderers before returning to Scotland. He had spells with Clyde, Albion Rovers, Ayr United, Hamilton Academical and St Johnstone before a knee injury cut short his career at the age of 24. Instead, he made his name as a manager. Evans – who was working in sales during the interim between playing and managing – kicked off his career with Stamford, winning a league title with the non-league outfit. One thing was abundantly clear – he was a winner.

The lure of a shiny new stadium, a club with designs on the second tier and a fresh challenge was too good for him to turn down and it was announced that Evans would succeed former manager Andy Scott, who left the club sitting 11th in the table when he was sacked. For what felt like long enough, Rotherham United were a team quite literally all over the place – playing in Sheffield at the Don Valley Stadium and training in neighbouring Doncaster while operating out of a warehouse on an industrial estate in Rotherham, which served as a base for the Millers' main offices, club shop and everything in between. Finally, they were coming out of the other side and a once broken football club was being pieced back together again. It allowed Evans to focus his efforts on what happened on the pitch.

Indeed, it was a recipe for success for the Scot, who brought about an end to Rotherham's longest-ever stint in the fourth tier of English football. History repeated itself when the Millers sealed successive promotions between 2012 and 2014, as they had back in the early 2000s when Ronnie Moore took the club from Division Three to Division One in the space of two years.

For many outsiders, the lasting image of Evans as the Rotherham boss is the famous clip of the Scot sprinting out of his technical area and down the touchline at Wembley after Alex Revell equalised against Leyton Orient in spectacular style in the League One play-off final. The camera caught Evans – who was just as taken aback as the 20,000 Millers fans packed into Wembley by Revell's split-second decision to take aim from around 35 yards out – with his arms in the air celebrating the goal which made it 2-2 before quickly composing himself and fixing his trousers, which had slipped down in his haste to join in with the supporters in their celebrations.

However, for Rotherham fans, his legacy was so much more than those ten seconds of unbridled passion. Evans did what he does best and after placing second in League Two in his first season in charge to secure automatic promotion, Rotherham scaled the Football League as they experienced the unbeatable feeling of winning the play-offs the following year.

Similarly, the sight of Evans dressed in beach attire, complete with a sombrero, a pair of colourful board shorts, flip-flops and the sunglasses to match – as if the Rotherham manager was ready to step straight out of the dugout at Elland Road and on to a plane to warmer climes – on the final day of the 2014/15 season is ingrained in many football fans' brains, for better or for worse. A social media campaign, which saw supporters circulate the hashtag #SombreroForSteve, saw Evans keep his promise to the Millers faithful to wear his best summer gear away at Leeds United for the last game of the term as Rotherham fans got into the party mood after securing their Championship status for another season.

It was a bittersweet moment when one of the most successful managers in Rotherham's history headed for the door, but it served as a reminder that the Millers had been fortunate enough to see the good times return in recent years thanks to the Scot. A Marmite manager – as some might say – love him or hate him, Evans holds a special place in the hearts of supporters after helping the club to rediscover its identity.

The feeling appeared to be mutual, too. As it happened, when Evans and Rotherham parted in 2015, it wasn't quite the long goodbye that everybody had foreseen. Over the course of the last decade since the two parties went their separate ways, Evans spoke highly of his abiding relationship with Rotherham chairman Stewart at every given opportunity, revealing he still kept in contact with him.

For all those reasons and more, when it was announced that Evans would be returning to the New York Stadium for a second stint in charge of the club on a Wednesday afternoon in April 2024, to say it gave the club a much-needed pick-me-up would be an understatement. Already relegated from the Championship after a disastrous 2023/24 league campaign, it was too late for Evans to save them this time but his presence in the dugout for the final three games of the season would give the club something they had been in short supply of – hope.

His achievements since leaving the club, most notably with Stevenage, spoke for themselves. Evans took Boro – a team on the brink of relegation from the EFL when he stepped into the breach in March 2022 – up to League One the following season and they spent the best part of the 2023/24 campaign challenging for the play-offs before he departed. His successes had already sparked rumours of a possible return to South Yorkshire midway through the season, but the club eventually landed their man.

Saturday, 19 September 2015
New York Stadium
EFL Championship
Rotherham United 2 (Odjidja-Ofoe 43', Connolly OG 90+3')
Cardiff City 1 (Whittingham 45')
Regardless of the fact he would later return, Evans's exit in September 2015 brought about the end of an era for Rotherham. Winless in seven with their only victory of the season coming against Cambridge United – a side ranked two divisions lower than Rotherham – in the League Cup, the Millers' poor start to the term meant they had some catching up to do. Evans's side were bottom of the Championship with just two points on the board but, fortunately, the teams around them – which included the likes of Bristol City, Preston North End, Bolton Wanderers and MK Dons – were also finding wins hard to come by.

The dismissal of Cardiff City keeper David Marshall in the first half of the game didn't hurt Rotherham's chances. The stopper was adjudged to have kicked out at Matt Derbyshire before being issued his marching orders by referee Keith Hill and the Bluebirds were forced into an early substitution to bring on Simon Moore.

Norwich City loanee Vadis Odjidja-Ofoe stepped up to take the resulting penalty, confidently finding the bottom left-hand corner. Just before half-time, the second penalty of the game was awarded to Cardiff following a foul by goalscorer Odjidja-Ofoe and Peter Whittingham levelled proceedings for the visitors.

With the last throw of the dice, substitute Chris Maguire sent a cross in from the right which crept in, taking a touch off Cardiff's Matt Connolly to make it 2-1 to Rotherham in the third minute of added time. It was a first defeat on the road for the Bluebirds but for Rotherham, it seemed as though things might finally be looking up.

Four days later, Richard Wood signed a one-month loan deal with League One side Fleetwood Town – where he linked up with former Millers David Ball and Jamie Proctor – after a 'frustrating' start to the season at Rotherham. After signing for the club from Charlton Athletic ahead of their return to the Championship in the summer of 2014, the defender was surplus to requirements.

It appeared unlikely that he would be seen in a Rotherham shirt again, with his contract due to expire at the end of the campaign. It's hard now to conceive of a different path for Wood, who would go on to leave in 2023 as a club legend after nine years on the Millers' books with three promotions, one EFL Trophy triumph, two Wembley goals and his own song to his name.

'Loads of times I thought I had to go and that it wasn't right,' Wood explains. 'It's weird how football can change so quickly. I never gave up and always had the mentality to stay professional and keep going. That's why I went out on loan to lower league clubs just to get games because I knew it might change at some point. You get low points and they were definitely low points.'

The future cult hero hadn't been involved since the beginning of the term and, later in October after his agreement with Fleetwood ended, the defender headed out again, this time to Chesterfield, for a further three months. His time would come for Rotherham that same season – he just didn't know it.

Saturday, 26 September 2015
St Andrew's Stadium
EFL Championship
Birmingham City 0
Rotherham United 2 (Derbyshire 32', Andreu 64')
It all came full circle for Evans upon his return to the club in April 2024 when it happened that his first game back in charge of Rotherham in his second stint would see the Millers lock horns with relegation rivals Birmingham City. Given that – unbeknownst at the time – his last game in charge during his first stint was against the Blues, it was almost as though the boss picked up where he left off.

But in September 2015, it was another performance to be proud of as Rotherham came away 2-0 winners at St Andrew's. It also saw the return of Kirk Broadfoot, who was named on the bench and available for selection for the first time since April 2015 after serving his suspension. With 32 minutes gone, Derbyshire rippled the net for the first time since the opening day of the season to give Rotherham the lead against his former club as the visitors' early pressure paid off. The Millers were eyeing a first win over the Blues since 1989 and Tony Andreu set them firmly on their way to victory after the break. After doing the hard work to win back the ball in a dangerous area, the midfielder made it 2-0 to put Rotherham in a commanding position.

The timing of Evans's dismissal took almost everyone by surprise. Rotherham had registered consecutive wins – something they hadn't even managed in 2014/15 when they stayed up in their first season in the Championship – and peeled themselves off the bottom of the table.

Blues academy graduate Joe Newell says: 'We kind of thought he was going to get the bullet but then, because we won two in a row, we thought "Oh, we've picked up now." We beat Cardiff at home and we beat Birmingham away. Then he got sacked, so Tony Stewart had obviously decided regardless of those two results.

'I remember beating Blues because I'm a big Birmingham fan and it was the first time I played there, so it was a massive day for me and my mates. We won 2-0 and had a great day. The gaffer in the changing room after was really happy and really bouncy and bubbly. It had been a really good week for us. He was probably thinking we were settled now we'd got a bit of momentum to try and kick on. I was quite surprised, to be honest.'

League table:

Position	*Club*	*Pl*	*GD*	*Pts*
20	Rotherham United	9	-6	8
21	Bolton Wanderers	9	-6	8
22	Preston North End	9	-4	7
23	MK Dons	9	-5	7
24	Bristol City	9	-8	6

However, on 28 September, a statement released by the club confirmed that Evans and Rotherham had parted company. It read: 'Following a meeting between the chairman and manager this morning, it was decided Rotherham United Football Club would part company with first team manager Steve Evans and his assistant Paul Raynor.

'During the said meeting, it became clear that both parties at the present time wished to head in a different direction. The meeting was at all times positive, constructive and straightforward. It was clear that the chairman and the management team only wanted what they felt was best for Rotherham United Football Club.

'The club would like to place on record our thanks to Steve and Paul for their huge contribution over the last three-and-a-half years. It has been simply an incredible journey. Moving on, Eric Black will assume first team duties for the time being. It has all come as a surprise but Rotherham United must move forward and the search for a new first team manager will begin immediately.'

It came as just as much of a blow to the players but all they could do was carry on doing what was asked of them and take courage from the two recent results, which had put a spring in their step and imbued some much-needed confidence.

'It was the first time we won two games in a row since we got promoted to the Championship. We went the full season [in 2014/15] without winning two games in a row and we somehow managed to stay up, which is an unbelievable stat really,' Richie Smallwood says. 'We hadn't won in eight games and that's a long time. You think "Bloody hell, somewhere along that line, somebody would get the sack." After winning two games, one at home and one away, you'd think it's time to get going. It was strange timing and probably a bit rare.'

Speaking to BBC Radio Sheffield, Evans said: 'I think when the chairman Tony Stewart and myself woke up yesterday morning, there was nothing on our radar. We had our normal meeting, as we have had on a daily basis for three-and-a-half years. The meeting was more business than anything else.'

However, he claimed the pair realised they were headed in different directions and, after an emotional conversation, Evans and Stewart hugged it out before agreeing to go their separate ways.

'I was out of the team circle at the time and we heard rumours that he might leave, but I didn't buy into that because I thought it was just rumours, but then he did,' Broadfoot says. 'It was more of a mutual thing that him and the chairman decided it was time for a change.'

It didn't take long for the rumour mill to start turning. Evans was among the favourites with the bookies to take up the vacancy at Doncaster Rovers, who were without a manager after the sacking of Paul Dickov earlier in the month. Whether there was any truth to the links or not, nothing came to fruition on that front. His name was also in the frame for a handful of roles in his native Scotland, but Evans and Raynor opted to hold out for something better later down the line.

* * *

Initially installed as the club's first-team coach in July by Evans, stand-in boss Eric Black found himself in the hotseat come September following the departure of the Millers' manager. He had arrived from Wigan Athletic to join Rotherham's set-up as Evans assembled his backroom team ahead of the new season and the manager was hoping Black's experience would be key. The former Aberdeen and FC Metz striker was perhaps best known for scoring as a 19-year-old in the 1983 European Cup Winners' Cup Final against Real Madrid. Under Sir Alex Ferguson, Aberdeen would go on to win the showpiece 2-1 in extra time.

Black made his first foray into coaching with Scottish giants Celtic as assistant manager to ex-England international John Barnes before branching out on his own with Motherwell and Coventry City. However, he was no stranger to stepping in as caretaker when Rotherham chairman Tony Stewart handed him the reins on an interim basis midway through the 2015/16 season. It would be the sixth time that the 52-year-old – who said he was 'flattered' to take up the position – had deputised at a club, having done so previously at the likes of Birmingham City, Sunderland and Blackburn Rovers.

'With the success that we had under Steve, we felt that he wasn't going to get sacked but unfortunately, in football, results happen and it changes a lot of things,' Lee Frecklington explains. 'We had a great time under him, so we were disappointed to see him leave. It creates that problem then of who is going to come next. Eric Black took over as interim for a while, which isn't ideal because you want some stability, and we didn't really know what was going on.'

Black had to put those doubts to the back of his mind with Sean Dyche's promotion-chasing Burnley due in town for his first game in charge. Despite the departure of Evans, the Millers had consecutive victories under their belt and something to take belief from, although it was difficult to feel that way.

Friday, 2 October 2015
New York Stadium
EFL Championship
Rotherham United 1 (G. Ward 75')
Burnley 2 (Gray 9', Vokes 81')

Where did the New York Stadium originate from and who chose its somewhat unusual name? That is often the question on the lips of opposing fans, especially those who have never visited Rotherham's new home, and Burnley were first-time visitors to the ground. The two teams hadn't gone head-to-head since 2004/05 – the season which brought about the Millers' downfall from the Championship.

While many hypothesised that the New York Stadium derived its name from the desire to simply bring some of the glitz and glamour of the Big Apple to Rotherham's patch in South Yorkshire, the real reason had much more logic behind it. It was revealed that the ground, which officially opened its doors for a pre-season friendly against Barnsley in July 2012, was named after the Guest and Chrimes Foundry – the company that occupied the site before the land was purchased by the club – which made the iconic fire hydrants that can still be seen on the streets of New York City.

Even more fascinating for visitors to the town is the sight of the club's former home, Millmoor, and its proximity to the New York Stadium. The derelict structure is still standing, just a stone's throw away from the club's new ground, despite Rotherham vacating the premises – which saw seven promotions and eight relegations – in 2008. But while some away fans might take a wander over the road to relive the past, the Millers were very much looking to the future – one they hoped might have Championship football in it.

Four days after the departure of Evans, the visit of Burnley would spell defeat for Black in his one and only game in charge before Rotherham moved to appoint a permanent figurehead. Perhaps unsurprisingly, there was a gulf in quality between the two teams. That Friday night saw Joey Barton make his full debut for the Lancashire outfit after signing for Burnley from newly relegated Queens Park Rangers, while Clarets captain Tom Heaton was fresh off the back of an England call-up from Roy Hodgson.

When the ball found its way through to striker Andre Gray in the seventh minute, he made no mistake to fire Burnley into the lead. However, Rotherham conjured up a moment of magic when Grant Ward equalised for the hosts in the second period. With 75 minutes gone, the Tottenham Hotspur loanee picked up the ball on the edge of the area and, after weighing up his options, decided to let fly from 25 yards out. It was a worthy winner of the club's goal of the season accolade.

'That was my first goal in the Championship, so I won't forget that one,' Ward remembers. 'It was quite a tough game because they were one of the top teams in the league. It was quite an open game and I was playing on the wing. Eric Black was the manager and he put me in the middle for a bit and told me to express myself. I was on the edge of the box and I got one-v-one with Joey Barton and I thought if I could get a few yards then I'd have a go.'

Unfortunately, the strike was cancelled out when Burnley's Sam Vokes bundled the ball over the line to make it 2-1 to the Clarets with less than ten minutes remaining. It wasn't the outcome Black or Rotherham were hoping for and the caretaker boss declined to comment on whether he was interested in being considered for the role on a full-time basis.

'It's a hard one to put your finger on,' Broadfoot explains. 'Some of the players that came in were really experienced, good players at Championship level. We got off to a bad start and we got into that mentality of having no confidence and the slightest wee mistake ended up in conceding a goal. It was one of those things.'

The players were left with a lingering feeling of disappointment after that result, with Rotherham made to wait until the two-week-long international break was over to right those wrongs. The club as a whole were in need of some stability moving forward and they needed to act fast.

Chapter Four

Changing the Game

IT TOOK Rotherham United chairman Tony Stewart little over a week to identify Steve Evans's successor. With the international break right around the corner, it bought the Millers chief the time he needed to narrow down the pool of applicants vying to be the next Rotherham boss to one final candidate: Neil Redfearn.

Just two days prior to his appointment in October 2015, it had been confirmed that the Millers had seen an approach for Walsall manager Dean Smith rejected. The West Midlands team, who were chasing promotion from League One at the time, made it clear that Rotherham's interest in Smith – who led the Saddlers to their first-ever Wembley appearance in the EFL Trophy Final in 2014/15 – was a non-starter.

A statement on Walsall's official website read: 'In response to media speculation, the club can confirm it received an approach from a Championship club for permission to speak to Dean Smith. This approach was categorically rejected. As one of the longest serving managers in the country, Dean has been instrumental in the club's progress since his appointment and is fundamental to our future plans.'

However, former Leeds United boss Redfearn stood out among over 60 other applicants to land the role, penning a two-and-a-half-year deal at the New York Stadium. Stewart highlighted the 50-year-old's wealth of coaching experience, including a stint managing in the Championship with the

Whites, and an illustrious playing career which saw him compete at the highest level as the reasoning for his choice. It was said that he ticked all the boxes and that it was a unanimous decision by the club.

Redfearn was among the top ten appearance-makers in English football, clocking up in excess of 1,000 games, with his most notable spell coming down the road at Barnsley, where he won promotion to the Premier League in 1996/97. On Redfearn's part, Stewart and Rotherham made a pleasant change from the events unfolding at Elland Road under Massimo Cellino's stewardship.

For Millers fans looking to do some research into their new boss and his coaching credentials, they could trace his roots way back to 2009 when – having balanced his late playing career with management – Dewsbury-born Redfearn first joined Leeds' academy set-up, initially linking up with the under-18s and then the reserve side. Redfearn, who had been involved with the West Yorkshire club in some capacity for around seven years, had three separate spells as caretaker boss. He initially took temporary charge following the departure of Simon Grayson in February 2012 before picking up where Neil Warnock left off in April 2013.

He was introduced to the first-team fold by Brian McDermott, balancing his position as a coach with the senior squad alongside his responsibilities to the youth team. When McDermott departed in May 2014, he returned to his role as academy manager. However, after McDermott's replacement Dave Hockaday's 70-day stint as Leeds boss came to an end, it fell to Redfearn to fill the void, registering three wins and a draw before stepping aside once more.

It wasn't until October that year that Redfearn was finally given his chance to take charge of his boyhood team on a permanent basis, replacing former head coach Darko Milanič. The decision was confirmed later in November by owner Cellino, with Redfearn requesting that a clause be added to his contract whereby he could return to his academy role at Thorp Arch if things didn't work out as planned with the first team. As it happened, he lasted 33 games in charge as head coach, with a record of 11 wins, 7 draws and 15 defeats.

When Uwe Rösler was announced as Leeds' new head coach in May 2015, Redfearn – whose relationship with Cellino had soured – opted to hand in his notice in July and by October, he found himself back in work at the New York Stadium as the new Rotherham manager. The 21st-placed Millers had just eight points on the board and the brief was simple: to keep the club in the Championship.

However, Redfearn had bigger ideas. Upon being unveiled as the new Millers boss, he appealed to the supporters' wildest dreams when he spoke of not just keeping the club in the second tier but, one day, taking them all the way to the Premier League. Redfearn cited Barnsley and Bournemouth, as examples. The Cherries had secured the Championship title in 2014/15 to ascend to the top flight for the first time in the club's history. Not to mention that the Cherries had been in a similar predicament to Rotherham back in 2008/09 when both clubs were issued a 17-point deduction before their League Two campaigns had even got under way. Redfearn was full of praise for the facilities at Rotherham, the club's owner, Stewart, and the players at his disposal, who he believed could help the Millers get to the top flight one day if they wanted it badly enough. For the time being, though, they needed to avoid taking one step back to take two steps forward if they were to make that dream a reality.

It was clear that Redfearn's strengths lay in coaching the stars of the future. Credited with overseeing the development of the likes of future England internationals Kalvin Phillips and Lewis Cook, along with players such as Sam Byram and

Alex Mowatt, he outlined his plans to bring Rotherham's promising talent to the fore and asserted that he aimed to 'change the face of Rotherham'.

'We want better quality youngsters and more players that fit into that category,' he told the club's official website upon his unveiling. 'We want to build a side around youth and legs, with some experience amongst it. We've done great to get to this level and now we're short, so we need to adjust and develop something that is sustainable, so we don't have to go through this process again.'

There would also be continuity as Redfearn confirmed that fitness coach Paul Warne – the future Rotherham boss – and goalkeeping coach Andy Dibble would be staying put. It was clear there was a longer-term project embedded in Redfearn's appointment, with the new man given a deal until the end of the 2017/18 season. However, time was very much of the essence in this instance.

Saturday, 17 October 2015
Griffin Park
EFL Championship
Brentford 2 (Judge 2', 57')
Rotherham United 1 (Mattock 46')
Just over a week later, fans had the chance to offer their verdict on the new boss when Rotherham travelled to Griffin Park, with Brentford away up next in their Championship schedule. It was the first of three games in the space of six days for the Millers, who would take on Reading during midweek before welcoming Sheffield Wednesday to the New York Stadium the following weekend.

In his first game in charge, Redfearn played it safe, making only minor adjustments to the side that lost to Burnley under Eric Black. It was a chance for players to step up and impress the new boss.

'There's always that natural reaction,' accepts keeper Lee Camp. 'How's a new manager going to see you? Are you going to be a part of his plans? Will this result in game time or no game time?

'Usually, it's your number nines and number ones that are the key positions. Managers seem to want to find some trust in a striker that can score a goal and a goalkeeper that can make a save and win them games. You feel that that's the nature of the beast. You're a little bit vulnerable. I was in pretty good form – I know I'd only had a couple of games – and I'd started pretty well that year having come into the club.'

There was a slight upturn in the mood around the club but, despite that new manager feeling – which can quickly wear off – it took just 67 seconds for Rotherham to fall behind against Brentford when Alan Judge volleyed home. After the break, Joe Mattock got Rotherham right back in it with an effort to match Judge's opener as the defender took aim from 20 yards. However, Judge headed Brentford back in front to bag a brace and it finished 2-1 in West London.

Redfearn was slightly glum-faced, while Brentford's Lee Carsley recorded his first victory in charge of the club. Fans might have been able to overlook the result, given that Redfearn was still getting his feet under the table, but what they really needed was someone to come in and hit the ground running.

Tuesday, 20 October 2016
New York Stadium
EFL Championship
Rotherham United 1 (Collins 48')
Reading 1 (Blackman 26')
A home clash against Reading triggered a flashback to a night that still very much felt as though it was only yesterday. A 2-1 win over the Royals on home soil in April 2015, courtesy

of goals from Matt Derbyshire and Lee Frecklington, had secured the club's place in the Championship for the 2015/16 season, relegating Millwall and Wigan Athletic in the process. The survival-winning squad soaked up a rapturous round of applause as chants of 'We are staying up' rang out around the New York Stadium. But the current crop – some of whom had played their part in keeping the club in the division – was at risk of frittering away their efforts.

After slipping to defeat against Brentford, the Rotherham manager opted to make changes to his side for the visit of Reading. Mattock, Richie Smallwood, Aidy White and Chris Maguire dropped out of the team to make way for Grant Ward, Tony Andreu, Tom Thorpe and Redfearn's newest recruit, loan signing Harry Toffolo, who came straight into the side just a day after joining the club.

The second-placed Royals were on a four-game winning streak in the league, with just one defeat in their last ten Championship outings, and they showed their quality 26 minutes in when Nick Blackman broke the deadlock with a stunning strike from range to make it ten goals in as many games. When the teams reappeared after the interval, Rotherham's stand-in skipper Danny Collins, donning the armband in the absence of the injured Frecklington, came up with an immediate reply. From a corner kick, the unmarked defender slotted home the leveller.

The returning Thorpe – who hadn't started a game since the opening day – spurned a chance to win it for the Millers with 15 minutes left and it finished 1-1 at the New York. Rotherham remained in the relegation zone, yet to break into double figures for the campaign, while the result saw Reading – hailed by Redfearn as the best side in the league – drop to third.

'You could already tell he was trying to put his stamp on things, which is difficult in such a short amount of time,' says

Farrend Rawson, who was favoured by Redfearn during his time at the club. 'He was good for me because he came from coaching Leeds' under-23s and he'd dealt with a lot of young players. He understood the youngsters and how to get the best out of people. As well as a manager, he was a great guy. All the lads could see that. He spoke to me a lot and tried to help me to improve my game in all different ways. He put faith in me and stuck with me.

'For the younger lads who were there at the time – and there were quite a few of us – it was good for us. We knew it wasn't going to be the old cliché of experience. It was going to be, if you play well, you play. He was a bit more of a tactician than Steve Evans, but all managers have different qualities, both positives and negatives.'

Friday, 23 October 2015
New York Stadium
EFL Championship
Rotherham United 1 (Thorpe 90+5')
Sheffield Wednesday 2 (Joao 46', Forestieri 50')
Prior to Rotherham's return to the Championship in 2014/15, the Millers and the Owls hadn't locked horns in the league since January 2003. There were some noteworthy nights in the League Cup from a Rotherham perspective in the interim, but the Millers were keen to take back the local bragging rights in front of a sold-out crowd in the second tier.

Earlier in the year, when the Owls last visited the New York in March 2015, the Millers were despondent by the time the full-time whistle put them out of their misery. After playing out a goalless draw at Hillsborough in the first half of the 2014/15 campaign, Rotherham found themselves 2-1 up in the 87th minute in the rematch. Ben Pringle had opened the scoring for the hosts in the second period and, after Caolan Lavery equalised with five minutes left to play, Bowery went straight down the other end 90 seconds later as Rotherham restored their lead.

However, two injury-time goals for Wednesday resulted in a 3-2 defeat. Atdhe Nuhiu made it 2-2 in the 93rd minute and the Owls weren't done there. Kieran Lee popped up with a 98th-minute winner to break Rotherham hearts. It was a result the Millers were eager to avenge when the Sky cameras came to town seven months later. The stage was set for Redfearn to lay claim to his first win as Rotherham boss – or so everyone hoped.

The Millers weren't without openings in the first half but what they didn't anticipate was the manner in which Wednesday would fly out of the blocks in the second half. Lucas João produced one of the easiest finishes of his career and the Owls doubled their advantage when Fernando Forestieri found himself in the right place at the right time to tap home and make it 2-0 to Sheffield Wednesday.

From then on, it was all the Owls and Rotherham were on the back foot. Thorpe did manage to grab a lifeline in the fifth minute of added time, but it was nothing more than a consolation. The result consigned Rotherham to a third defeat in four games and Redfearn's wait for three points went on. The only positive was the atmosphere inside the New York Stadium that day, which was as loud as it had ever been. Now, all the players needed to do was give the fans something to cheer about.

Saturday, 31 October 2015
Pride Park
EFL Championship
Derby County 3 (Weimann 7', Butterfield 45', Keogh 76')
Rotherham United 0
By the time Redfearn had got the lay of the land, it became evident that the boss needed to inject some new blood in

the transfer window. Until then, he would have to rely on free agents and loan deals to get them through to January as a temporary fix. The Millers manager made some smart moves. Leon Best began training with the club and would unwittingly play a big part in the reverse fixture against Derby County towards the tail end of the term. At one stage, Rotherham had former West Ham United forward Ricardo Vaz Tê – who would instead put pen to paper with relegation rivals Charlton – and ex-Manchester City youngster Adam Drury, whose next club ended up being non-league Gainsborough Trinity, training with them. Potential permanent targets began to do the rounds, too, as the club were linked with Hibernian and Scotland under-21s striker Jason Cummings.

Redfearn was also well aware that some of his existing players would need to make way for fresh faces. That included Richard Wood, who headed back out on loan to League One side Chesterfield almost immediately after his emergency agreement with Fleetwood Town expired.

And as Halloween rolled around, Rotherham were in for a fright when they made the journey to Pride Park. A 3-0 defeat saw Redfearn's team hit rock bottom. Austrian international Andreas Weimann opened his account for the Rams within seven minutes. On the stroke of half-time, Derby's summer signing Jacob Butterfield followed suit, rifling in a shot from outside the box to make it 2-0 to the hosts, giving the Millers plenty to mull over in the changing room at the break.

Long-serving defender Richard Keogh gave Rotherham little chance of getting back into the game when he made it 3-0 – his first goal in almost two years – to all but wrap up the points. Worryingly, it could have been more and Redfearn pulled no punches in his post-match press conference. The Millers manager identified the 'lack of workrate and wanting to win' as his team's downfall, urging the players to 'take responsibility' for a result that saw his side drop to the foot of the table.

It was now four defeats and a draw for Redfearn, whose side had downed tools after falling behind. They certainly didn't look like a team that had the strength of character to recover from a three-goal deficit – much more on that later.

League table:

Position	*Club*	*Pl*	*GD*	*Pts*
20	MK Dons	14	-9	11
21	Bristol City	14	-10	11
22	Bolton Wanderers	14	-10	10
23	Charlton Athletic	14	-13	10
24	Rotherham United	14	-12	9

Tuesday, 3 November 2015
Riverside Stadium
EFL Championship
Middlesbrough 1 (Downing 16')
Rotherham United 0

The Millers could have done without a trip to another top-six side in their quest for much-needed points, but such was the nature of the division's relentless fixture schedule. While they weren't having much luck on the pitch to show for it, the players were experimenting with a new system and a new style of play which would inevitably bring its challenges. One member of the Rotherham squad enjoying the task was former Middlesbrough man Smallwood, who was relishing his Riverside homecoming.

'I grew up at the Middlesbrough academy and everyone knows what an amazing academy it is – probably one of the best in the country throughout the years developing England internationals – so I was always seen as having a technical upbringing,' Smallwood explains. 'When I came to Rotherham, it wasn't quite that, but it also suited my game.

'It was nice to have a change-up of the style of play, trying to pass through the lines and play through the thirds. He [Neil Redfearn] kept telling me how good I was and told me all the different passes I could play. I owe him a big thanks, really, because he was the first manager that probably did that.

'He was probably the one manager before I went to Hull that gave me the most confidence in my play, really. The results didn't come off which was a shame, because everyone was enjoying the style of football.'

However, it wasn't meant to be against Boro. Stewart Downing – someone Smallwood had just missed out on playing with during his stint at the club – scored the only goal of the game in a 1-0 win for the hosts. Redfearn had his rational head on when speaking after the game, admitting that it was 'not the Middlesbroughs of this world' where Rotherham were likely to pick up results. However, with Ipswich Town – who would narrowly miss out on a play-off spot come May – up next, there appeared to be few opportunities where the Millers could realistically put points on the board.

Saturday, 7 November 2015
New York Stadium
EFL Championship
Rotherham United 2 (Barker 56', Derbyshire 59')
Ipswich Town 5 (Pitman 8', Douglas 22', Murphy 43' ,48' ,72')
One point from a possible 15 and bottom of the pile wasn't where Redfearn wanted to be a month into his tenure as Rotherham manager. All the Millers could do was look ahead to the next game. They were back on home turf for the visit of Ipswich Town and, although they managed to get on the scoresheet this time, once again they were outclassed.

Less than ten minutes in, they were fighting a losing battle. Brett Pitman gave the Tractor Boys the lead and the Millers had their heads in their hands. There was a collective groan from the home fans when they went 2-0 down through Jonathan Douglas. Before half-time, Daryl Murphy had Ipswich 3-0 up and cruising at the New York. Even Redfearn didn't blame the home fans for booing the players off the pitch at the interval as discontent set in. And just three minutes after the restart, it went from bad to worse when Murphy put himself on a brace and the Millers 4-0 down with no way back.

Rotherham's new loan signing from Manchester City, Brandon Barker, had a trick up his sleeve. The 19-year-old winger was thrown in at the deep end, with Redfearn naming Barker in the starting line-up for his debut, and he gave supporters a taste of what he could do when he unleashed a curling effort into the top corner.

On the hour mark, a chance presented itself to Derbyshire when he lashed the ball home from a difficult angle on the volley and the frustrations on the pitch could be felt in that strike. But Murphy made sure that all three points and the match ball were going back to Suffolk when he sealed his first career hat-trick in the 72nd minute to make it 5-2.

Rotherham were in unwanted possession of the Championship's worst defensive record, conceding 33 goals while scoring only 17, and if they didn't plug their leaky defence sooner rather than later, there would be no hope of survival. Meanwhile, Redfearn insisted he wanted his players 'to grow up and become men and take responsibility'. After the hammering by Ipswich, the next test was one that would surely be playing on his mind.

Saturday, 21 November 2015
Elland Road
EFL Championship
Leeds United 0
Rotherham United 1 (Newell 54')

There was an extra bite to the Yorkshire derby at Elland Road for both clubs when Rotherham went head-to-head with Leeds United. A month earlier, the Whites had announced Steve Evans as their new head coach. The former Rotherham boss had been out of work for just under a month after parting ways with the Millers and his next managerial role took even him by surprise.

'Perhaps I wouldn't be the chosen manager for many Leeds United fans,' he told the club's official website as he asked Leeds supporters to give him the 'benefit of the doubt'. Joined by his assistant, Paul Raynor, on a rolling contract, Evans had given the club a pick-me-up after Leeds found themselves in a mid-season slump, losing three games on the bounce before the former Rotherham boss came in.

The last time Millers supporters had seen Evans at Elland Road, he was wearing a sombrero and a pair of funky board shorts but this time, he was dressed to impress in a suit with the Leeds United crest embroidered on the jacket. It was some turnaround. The West Yorkshire outfit had witnessed just one defeat in their last five outings, coming into the Rotherham clash on the back of consecutive victories over Cardiff City and Huddersfield Town. In the opposing dugout, Redfearn – who had essentially swapped places with Evans – was eager to get one over on his ex-employers, too. The Rotherham boss was fully aware that he had to act, making nine changes to the side that lost 5-2 to Ipswich.

Given the existing ties between the two clubs and their managers, it was always unlikely to be a fixture that would go off without a hitch. When Redfearn was denied a car parking space at Elland Road – with the Millers boss later explaining that fitness coach Paul Warne drove Redfearn's car to the stadium while he made other travel arrangements to find a way around what he described as a 'childish' situation – it could have detracted from what happened on the pitch that afternoon. However, he made sure his players blocked out the noise and stayed on task.

New signing Best, who joined Rotherham on a short-term deal until the end of the season, came into the side. Best hadn't found the back of the net since April 2014, when he scored in Sheffield Wednesday's 4-2 win over Bournemouth in the Championship, having been without a club since the end of the 2014/15 season when he was released by Blackburn Rovers. Stephen Kelly was also handed his debut. The former Republic of Ireland international was let go by Reading at the end of 2014/15 but Redfearn recognised just how important his know-how could be in the battle for survival.

The game also marked a welcome return for club captain Frecklington. The midfielder had been sidelined since September with a grade one calf injury and his ten-game absence had been felt, but the lifelong Leeds supporter wasn't about to miss this one. Added incentive came from the fact it was his dad's birthday and Frecklington made it a double celebration that afternoon.

He says: 'When you know you're facing a spell on the sidelines, I always look at the fixture list and pick a date and say, "That's the game I'm going to try everything to get back for." I remember looking at the list and thinking "Wow, Leeds away – that's the game I've got to be ready for." If I could relive any game in my career, it would be that one. It was my dad's 50th birthday and it was the Leeds away game, so I was desperate to get back fit for that because it was a big thing for my family. We won away 1-0 and it was a much-needed win.

'To stand in the front of the tunnel as captain of a team at a packed-out Elland Road, walking out to "Marching on Together", is definitely something I dreamed about. I don't know if he [Frecklington's dad] was happy with us winning, but he was delighted to see me play at Elland Road. Then we had a good party when we got back on the Saturday night.'

Redfearn's first win at the helm came against his former team and, like Frecklington, he couldn't have scripted a better return to West Yorkshire if he'd tried. After a relatively quiet first half, Joe Newell broke the deadlock for Rotherham with 54 minutes played. Smallwood picked out Newell, who buried his free header to give the Millers a 1-0 lead – the only goal of the game.

Both teams finished the contest with ten men after the mood came to a head in the second half. Best and Gaetano Berardi were caught up in an altercation after Best appeared to elbow Berardi. The Leeds man's reaction saw both players issued red cards by referee Keith Stroud and Best, who would have to serve a three-game ban as a result, and Berardi left the field with bloodied faces.

Leeds refused to give up but, despite throwing everything at Rotherham, it was to be Redfearn's day as the Millers moved off the foot of the table and registered their first victory at Elland Road since August 1962 in front of a crowd of over 25,000. The Millers manager – who had been vocal in the build-up to the game about how much he was relishing this one – insisted that his side 'wanted it more' and that the passion he had instilled in his players had been rewarded. The 900-plus Rotherham fans inside the stadium joined in a chorus of 'There's only one Neil Redfearn'.

League table:

Position	*Club*	*Pl*	*GD*	*Pts*
20	Charlton Athletic	17	-11	16
21	Huddersfield Town	17	-9	15
22	MK Dons	17	-9	15
23	Rotherham United	17	-15	12
24	Bolton Wanderers	17	-13	11

Saturday, 28 November 2015
New York Stadium
EFL Championship
Rotherham United 3 (Clarke-Harris 9', 27', Frecklington 75')
Bristol City 0

Redfearn was of the belief that victory over Leeds United could act as a 'catalyst' and it appeared he was right. For the first time since beating Cardiff and Birmingham under Evans in September, Rotherham secured back-to-back wins in the Championship. After seeing off Leeds at Elland Road, the Millers had a spring in their step and their next win came against fellow strugglers Bristol City.

Redfearn continued to put his own spin on the squad, making a double swoop for Luke Hyam and Simon Lenighan on the Friday before the game. Hyam, a midfielder, joined from his hometown club Ipswich Town. Lenighan was plucked from Leeds United's youth team, having skippered both the under-18s and under-21s under Redfearn. However, the latter would depart the club without making a single appearance. Lenighan's contract was suspended a week after signing 'pending an investigation into the matter' after pleading guilty to assaulting three women while on a night out in February.

In February 2016, a club statement confirmed: 'Following an internal investigation into the matters recently in the press and following the reported conduct of the player, Rotherham United can announce that it has terminated the contract of Simon Lenighan. The club will be making no further comment on this matter.'

Academy graduate Jerry Yates took his place on the bench against Bristol City after returning from his temporary spell at National League side Harrogate Town. The Millers recalled the striker to provide cover for injuries, while allowing fellow youngster Mason Warren to head out on loan to non-league outfit Sheffield FC. Attacker Maguire was also sent out to

Oxford United on a two-month deal as the summer signing turned elsewhere in search of game time.

The home side needed time to grow into the game but Jonson Clarke-Harris – who expressed after the match just how much he was enjoying life at the club – got Rotherham up and running by doing what he did best, cutting inside and taking aim from distance to open the scoring against the Robins. And when he had the chance to double his tally for the afternoon from the spot in the first half, after Kirk Broadfoot was bundled to the ground, he gratefully accepted. The forward – who could have had a hat-trick that afternoon – made no mistake from 12 yards. Frecklington made sure there was no coming back for the visitors when he made it 3-0 in the 75th minute to get off the mark for the season. Former Millers marksman Kieran Agard, now of Bristol City, posed a threat but Rotherham claimed another win and another clean sheet.

'He put a lot of trust in young players and he gave me the chance that I wanted,' Clarke-Harris says of Redfearn. 'I could make a mistake and he'd put an arm around me. I thought he was unbelievable. I thought he was class. He'd come from a big club like Leeds and you want to learn so much, but you want to impress at the same time.

'He took a lot of pressure off me. I'd make a mistake and he'd say "Look, don't worry about it. Just get it right the next time." He was helping me on the training ground and showing me what I should be doing and showing me what players that he'd worked with would do in that situation. He was easy to get along with and a pleasure to work with.'

Saturday, 5 December 2015
New York Stadium
EFL Championship
Rotherham United 1 (Newell 18')
Wolverhampton Wanderers 2 (Henry 5', Batth 44')

Rotherham were making a habit of coming up against former players and they were reunited with another familiar face in Adam le Fondre, who had been loaned out to Wolverhampton Wanderers by Cardiff City for the duration of the campaign. The striker scored 58 goals in 105 appearances for Rotherham between 2009 and 2011 in League Two before making the switch to Reading, where he won promotion to the Premier League. If anyone knew what the former Millers talisman was capable of, it was his ex-employer.

Wolves also had another Rotherham old boy in their ranks. On-loan Arsenal stopper Emi Martínez linked up with Kenny Jackett's side on a season-long loan but, after suffering an injury and finding himself unable to force his way back into the team upon his return, he failed to make the matchday squad.

On the back of victories over Leeds United and Bristol City, Rotherham had a third successive win in their sights, but Wolves were in need of three points, too. James Henry's early goal knocked the wind out of the home team. Newell snatched the opportunity to equalise in the 18th minute – his second goal in three games after netting the winner against Leeds. Regrettably, the visitors hit Rotherham right where it hurt on the stroke of half-time. Danny Batth's header restored Wolves' advantage, forcing the hosts to retreat.

Despite dominating the second period, Redfearn's side were unable to get back into the game due to some solid defending from the visitors. It was a frustrating afternoon for Rotherham, who passed up a chance to climb out of the bottom three.

Friday, 11 December 2015
Ewood Park
EFL Championship
Blackburn Rovers 1 (Hyam OG 30')
Rotherham United 0

There were differing feelings in the dugouts at Ewood Park. Paul Lambert, who had taken charge at Blackburn Rovers in November – around a month after Redfearn's arrival at Rotherham – had enjoyed a strong start and was about to claim his third win in four games and a first victory on home soil. Redfearn, on the other hand, was struggling to string together a consistent run of results.

Rotherham were without Danny Ward – who Redfearn had pinpointed as the man who could be the Millers' 20-goal-a-season striker if he put his mind to it – after he picked up an injury, while Luke Hyam came in for his full debut, having made appearances off the bench against Bristol City and Wolves. Hyam did get on the scoresheet but for the wrong team as he diverted the ball into his own net. It was the only goal of the game in a 1-0 win for Blackburn and, although the scoreline didn't necessarily reflect Rotherham's efforts, it was another defeat for the Millers.

There was little to write home about in the games against Wolves and Blackburn, except to note that the Millers could – and probably should – have been at least two points better off. Those two points could have put some distance between Rotherham and the bottom three.

Tuesday, 15 December 2015
John Smith's Stadium
EFL Championship
Huddersfield Town 2 (Carayol 31', Miller 73')
Rotherham United 0

Just three points separated Rotherham and David Wagner's Huddersfield Town ahead of another Yorkshire derby. On the pitch, however, the gulf in quality appeared much greater. A moment of individual brilliance from Mustapha Carayol opened the scoring, the winger beating Camp from 25 yards out. Half-time substitute Ishmael Miller made it 2-0 in the second half with a simple finish and when Hyam passed up an open goal, it just about summed up Rotherham's afternoon. The Millers slumped to a third straight defeat – it was now eight losses in Redfearn's first 11 games – and the boss was particularly critical of the players he had inherited.

'This squad of players isn't good enough at this level, it's as simple as that,' Redfearn said, pulling no punches. 'This is common knowledge. We are second from bottom, we just scraped by last year, probably didn't recruit very well in the summer. We let good players go – better players than what we have got. We brought in players who are sub-standard in the summer and now we are left with this. This might sound a bit harsh, but these are the facts.'

Former Millers manager Steve Evans responded to Redfearn's comments via the media as the two bosses found themselves at loggerheads over the situation.

'I could have said that here, couldn't I?' he said. 'But I have got too much professionalism about myself. I have read those comments and it just sounds like a man who is under extreme pressure and wonders what happens if he loses the next one.'

Saturday, 19 December 2015
New York Stadium
EFL Championship
Rotherham United 2 (Frecklington 28', Newell 57')
Hull City 0

Lee Frecklington exhaled as he waited for referee Eddie Ilderton to blow his whistle, readying himself to step up and take his penalty against Hull City in the 28th minute. But the midfielder already knew which way he was going to go to beat Allan McGregor and put Rotherham in front.

It was a moment 18 months in the making for Frecklington. On a summer's day in May 2014, encased on all sides by over 43,000 fans housed inside Wembley Stadium, the midfielder began the long walk up to the spot to take his turn in the shoot-out against Leyton Orient in front of the O's supporters. He was second on the list for Rotherham as the League One play-off final boiled down to penalties. Top scorer Kieran Agard had already slotted away his spot kick – no surprises there – before Lloyd James levelled things up for the O's to make it 1-1. Rotherham's season was riding on the tense shoot-out. It was a contest which called upon both mental and physical resolve and, according to Sky Sports commentator Daniel Mann, who narrated those agonising seconds, the man in question had plenty of that. 'The club's player of the year,' Mann said. 'A man they've been able to count on so often this season when it really matters.'

Having played through cramp sustained during the 30 minutes of extra time, Frecklington opted to place the ball to Orient keeper Jamie Jones's right, only for the stopper's outstretched palm to produce the first save of the shoot-out and put Rotherham on the back foot. Fortunately for him, the Millers would go on to win 4-3 on penalties and secure promotion back to the Championship after Ben Pringle, James Tavernier and Richie Smallwood all converted while Millers stopper Adam Collin produced two saves from Mathieu Baudry and, crucially, Chris Dagnall. Nevertheless, it had taken Frecklington some time to shake it off and when Rotherham were awarded a spot kick against the Tigers in December 2015, there was nobody who wanted it more than the club captain. The 30-year-old was never going to miss this time. He blasted the ball straight down the centre.

'I got a penalty against Hull at home and I was waiting for that after I missed the penalty at Wembley in the shoot-out in the play-off final,' he acknowledges. 'That was playing on my mind massively for a long time and I waited ages for another penalty. We got it against Hull and all I could think about was the Wembley one and how I had to score to try and put that right. I put the ball down and smashed it as hard as I could, so that was a big relief to put that Wembley hoodoo behind me.'

His relief was palpable as he hammered the ball into the roof of the net. The goal music began to ring out around the ground as Frecklington wheeled away with the ball in his hand, bestowing a kiss upon it.

On more than one occasion, Camp was called upon to spare Rotherham's blushes during the game and when Hull struck the upright, it was evident that the Millers would need another, if only to settle their nerves. It was Newell who put the icing on the cake in the second half as the winger made it 2-0, the ball rattling in off McGregor's crossbar.

It was a result which ended a run of three consecutive defeats. And if there was one player that summed up the Millers' will to win, it was Broadfoot. The Scottish defender was beginning to cement his cult hero status.

'The press officer said to me that I was huge with the fans on social media, but I don't have social media myself,' Broadfoot says. 'When we played Hull at home, there was loads of pictures going about of a brick wall with me next to it. I went out there and gave my best every game. I never left anything out on the pitch. I'd put my head in places people wouldn't put their feet and I wasn't afraid to get hurt while doing it.

'From my time at Rangers, I had a mentality that we needed to win every game and I took that when I went down south to Blackpool and then over to Rotherham. It's not nice being down in the bottom half, but you've got to be a wee bit realistic in the Championship.'

Both Camp and Mattock featured in *The Football League Paper*'s team of the day, while Redfearn was named as the top boss. It was deserved recognition for a fine performance against a team still very much in contention for automatic promotion.

Saturday, 26 December 2015
New York Stadium
EFL Championship
Rotherham United 4 (G. Ward 56', D. Ward 74', Newell 80', Clarke-Harris 86')
Bolton Wanderers 0

A Boxing Day outing during the Christmas period is something of a ritual for football fans up and down the country – as much a part of the annual tradition as a roast dinner or presents under the tree – but it also has the ability to make or break the festivities.

Bolton and Charlton comprised the Championship's bottom two; two former Premier League teams fighting to avoid the drop to League One. Wanderers – who had ex-England international Emile Heskey on their books – were rock bottom of the Championship and coming to terms with the fact that a season in the third tier of English football for the first time in 23 years was a very real possibility. Bolton's players were still awaiting their wages from November, with the club facing a winding-up petition from HMRC, but boss Neil Lennon explained after the game against Rotherham that they were due to be paid that same week.

As for the fixture itself, Redfearn's players looked sharp after spending part of Christmas Day on the training pitch, while Bolton were given the day off before travelling across to South Yorkshire on the morning of the game. The second half saw all the action after a goalless first 45 minutes. A well-worked corner routine saw Rotherham take the lead in the 56th minute through Grant Ward.

His namesake, Danny Ward, grabbed Rotherham's second of the afternoon after combining with Newell. With ten minutes remaining, Newell would go from provider to scorer when he netted a third for Rotherham as Wanderers simply collapsed. Rotherham weren't done there, either.

Clarke-Harris made it 4-0 late in the day to score his sixth goal of the season.

'That was a really good day at the office,' Rawson, who played the full 90 minutes, explains. 'It was snowing as well. It was my first proper stint in professional football where you have to watch what you eat. Normally for the younger lads, at Christmas it's not very busy and you get time off. It was the first time Christmas dinner looked a bit different and I had to ease up a bit on the dinner, which my mum wasn't too happy about. I was saying, "We've got Bolton tomorrow, so I can't eat too much!"'

The sight of goalkeeper Camp's fist cutting through the air became synonymous with Rotherham's fight for survival. At full time, the keeper would swivel on his heel and give the Millers supporters a fist pump as a show of triumph as they rallied behind the gesture.

'There was a bit of an ongoing joke with Kirk Broadfoot for a while that I did it and he was saying "Oh, you're giving it to the fans" and all that sort of stuff. Then it became a standing joke to wind him up, more than anything,' Camp laughs. 'I don't think he wanted to kill anybody as much as he wanted to kill me – the sinister in me got pleasure in winding him up.

'The fans feel it as well with you. They go through the roller-coaster ride of emotions. Sometimes, showing a bit of passion is not a bad thing. It's a bit of superstition, too. Once you do it once and you win, you can't not do it again. I would like to think that they saw that I was passionate and that I cared. It was a bit of emotion coming out at the fact we'd won a game. It was like a release.'

Exiting the relegation zone was the belated Christmas gift that all Millers fans had hoped for. Four wins in seven, as Redfearn said, was play-off form. However, the three straight defeats leading up to the game against Hull were part of the reason his team were still battling against the drop rather than challenging for promotion. Nevertheless, things appeared to be looking up for Rotherham United – until they weren't just three days later.

League table:

Position	*Club*	*Pl*	*GD*	*Pts*
20	MK Dons	23	-11	22
21	Rotherham United	23	-10	21
22	Bristol City	23	-17	21
23	Charlton Athletic	23	-19	19
24	Bolton Wanderers	23	-19	14

Chapter Five

Desperate Times

NATURALLY, THERE comes a point in the season when the infamous 'P-word' slips back into circulation. Permutations are rarely heard of – for obvious reasons – outside of the final couple of months of a campaign but when they are, you know it means the business end of the season is nearing. For Rotherham United, instead of possible scenarios in which they could get promoted – as had been the case in previous years under Steve Evans's stewardship – it would be about how many points would guarantee them Championship football the following season. During the 2016/17 campaign, when the Millers registered a record low points tally, they were relegated from the second tier as early as 1 April 2017. However, in 2015/16, their fate was still very much in their hands and the New Year brought with it fresh optimism.

The Millers had just started to find their groove under Neil Redfearn – registering back-to-back victories over Hull City and Bolton Wanderers – and they were hoping to see out 2015 on a high. A 4-0 triumph over relegation-threatened Bolton lifted the club out of the bottom three, but it was almost as if the football gods decided they were getting ahead of themselves.

A sobering defeat to Fulham – who had underperformed by their standards in the Championship – served as a stark reminder that they weren't yet out of the woods. The January transfer window couldn't come soon enough for Redfearn, who had previously criticised the squad bequeathed to him by Evans.

Tuesday, 29 December 2015
Craven Cottage
EFL Championship
Fulham 4 (Woodrow 6', 45', Kacaniklic 59', McCormack 69')
Rotherham United 1 (Rawson 20')
It sparked cause for concern when the first team to complete a league double over Rotherham made it look effortless. Newly appointed Fulham manager Slaviša Jokanović – who watched on as interim head coach Stuart Gray took charge for the final time – met his players just an hour before kick-off and whatever he said had the desired effect.

It all fell apart for Redfearn's men inside six minutes. A lapse in concentration allowed Cauley Woodrow to sneak in and round Lee Camp to slot home the opening goal. Rotherham were back on terms 15 minutes later through Farrend Rawson. Woodrow netted his second of the evening and Ross McCormack and Woodrow, a deadly duo on the night, linked up again in a move which ended in Alexander Kačaniklić sweeping home to make it 3-1 to the hosts. Rotherham midfielder Richie Smallwood sat on the byline looking deflated while the Cottagers celebrated what was already shaping up to be a comprehensive victory. McCormack eventually got in on the act to make it 4-1 and it was evident that Rotherham were finding it increasingly hard to compete.

'Fulham had McCormack and he was tough – he was on fire,' Rawson says. 'We played Burnley on TV on a Friday night and it was Andre Gray and Vokes up front. Sheffield Wednesday had Fernando Forestieri. My toughest game was Ipswich at home – they had Brett Pitman and Daryl Murphy.

'It was a really good experience playing against some top sides. Rotherham were a massive underdog in that league.

We were always favourites to go down but the lads thrived off it. It was like "Right, same again." The bookies, the papers and fans of other teams were saying "Rotherham are going to go down this year." It became a springboard to prove people wrong, to turn some heads and upset some people. We got brushed under the carpet. That never-say-die attitude ran through the whole of the club. We lost together and we won together. There was more pressure to stay up inside the camp than outside the camp.

'I had Kirk Broadfoot next to me, who was unbelievable for me. He was a class player on and off the ball. He was even helping me in games, getting me through games and teaching me stuff. I had Danny Collins as well, who had a vast amount of experience.'

In an effort to reassure supporters, Redfearn hinted at the forthcoming January transfer window, during which he could look to improve upon what he already had in the building and make some room for new players. The Rotherham boss revealed he had his targets in place and knew where he needed to strengthen but if the defeat to the Cottagers was anything to go by, all areas needed some work.

* * *

As the transfer window rolled around once again, it gave Redfearn the chance to put his own slant on the team. The direction the Rotherham boss wanted to go in was no secret, with Manchester City youngster Shay Facey the first player through the door at the beginning of the month. The 20-year-old, who had represented England at under-16s right through to under-20s level, was a versatile defender who spent the first half of the campaign on loan with City's sister team New York City in Major League Soccer.

The following week, the Millers announced the free transfers of defender Aymen Belaïd from Bulgarian side

Levski Sofia and goalkeeper Alex Cairns from Chesterfield. Belaïd, who was born in France but represented Tunisia on the national stage, had spells across Europe playing in France and Prague before moving to England. Cairns, on the other hand, was known to Redfearn from his time at Leeds United. The stopper signed a deal until the end of the season and his signature saw Adam Collin depart on loan. Another of Rotherham's Wembley heroes was heading for the door as the keeper joined Aberdeen, but the Millers would still need back-up in the goalkeeping department, which Cairns would provide.

'It's something that I always wanted to do during my career – to play games,' Collin explains. 'That's why I dropped into non-league eventually to play 220 games. I went to Carlisle and within a month into the start of the season, I was playing games and I played 150-odd games on the bounce for Carlisle. I signed for Rotherham and it wasn't long into the season that I replaced Scott Shearer as the number one and played all the games pretty much up until Emi Martínez and Lee Camp came in. Personally, it wasn't a great last season at Rotherham playing-wise. That's ultimately why it was my decision, but also the club's decision, to send me out on loan.'

January also saw the return of Leeds legend Luciano Becchio. The prolific frontman, who scored 86 goals in 221 appearances for the West Yorkshire club, had a brief loan stint with the Millers in 2014/15. Evans signed Becchio on a temporary deal from Norwich City in September 2014, but it was his relationship with Redfearn – which dated back to his time at Elland Road – that lured him back to the New York Stadium. After being released by Norwich, he returned to his native Argentina but had been training with Rotherham for several weeks prior to putting pen to paper on an agreement until May. Redfearn also used his connections to recruit Dewsbury-born midfielder Chris Dawson, who he brought through the Leeds academy. Dawson featured in the Championship under both Neil Warnock and Redfearn, signing for Rotherham after being released by the club.

Soon after, Nottingham Forest winger Chris Burke completed a loan move to the Millers, having played against them earlier in the season. Also joining on a temporary deal was Andrew Shinnie from Championship rivals Birmingham City, making it seven new additions in the January window.

As a result, there were several players deemed surplus to requirements. Aidy White had his contract cancelled by mutual consent, having spent time on loan at neighbouring Barnsley during the season. The 24-year-old – who made just ten appearances for Rotherham, six of which came off the bench – turned his loan with the Reds into a permanent transfer.

Meanwhile, Jordan Bowery, who made three appearances during a loan spell with Bradford City in League One, also left the club. The striker – formerly Rotherham's record signing – made 44 appearances in total, scoring six times. Bowery would join League Two club Oxford United after leaving the Millers. At the beginning of February, Chris Maguire joined Bowery at Oxford, having spent time on loan with the U's, and the pair would help the club win automatic promotion to League One that season.

Redfearn also had Richard Wood back in contention after the defender was recalled in December to give the Rotherham boss options, with Harry Toffolo developing a viral illness. Later in the month, a contractual issue surrounding Lewis Buxton – which kept the summer signing out of the side due to a clause which would have triggered an extension of his agreement – was resolved, although the defender wouldn't feature for the remainder of the season.

Rotherham were in need of a striker to bolster their attacking line-up and Redfearn revealed the club had made a 'tentative enquiry' to Cardiff City about re-signing Alex Revell. The striker, best remembered for his 'ambitious but brilliant' brace against Leyton Orient to seal promotion back to the Championship at Wembley in the 2014 League One play-off final, was a fan favourite at the New York Stadium. It wasn't necessarily his goals-to-games ratio that had earned him cult hero status. It was more his work ethic and commitment to the cause during his time at the club, although his 35-yard equaliser against Orient didn't hurt, with his famous slogan immortalised on T-shirts, mugs and all other forms of merchandise and mementos. Revell had been sold to the Bluebirds in January 2015, reuniting with former boss Russell Slade. After the player returned to the Welsh team following a short-term loan with Wigan Athletic in November 2015, Redfearn said Revell was a 'top player' he was interested in bringing back to the club, but nothing ever materialised.

Amid all the incomings and outgoings, another departure was confirmed when assistant boss Eric Black was offered 'an opportunity that he felt he couldn't turn down' according to manager Redfearn as the Rotherham coach left to become Rémi Garde's number two at Aston Villa.

'I have really enjoyed working at Rotherham and I have met and worked with some terrific individuals,' he told the club's official website. 'I didn't know Neil [Redfearn] before he arrived, but he was brilliant to me from day one. He is an exceptional coach, one of the best I have worked with, and with the support of the chairman and everyone else, I am sure he will take the club forward.'

Redfearn moved swiftly to appoint Nicky Eaden as his new assistant on a two-and-a-half-year contract. The pair had been team-mates at Barnsley when the Reds won promotion to the Premier League. More recently, he had been working with Leicester City's under-21s, bringing his four-year stint with the Foxes to an end to rejoin Rotherham, with the Sheffield-born coach having worked under former Millers boss Andy Liddell at the club in 2011.

Redfearn said upon his unveiling: 'When Danny Wilson became manager [at Barnsley], he started to put the kids in and I think my experience of seeing those young players coming through shaped my thinking about how you can develop and plan and build a team. Nicky was part of that process and he understands that as well. Also, he has extensive experience at this level. It's good for us to have him in.'

Now, Redfearn had his backroom team and his squad assembled. He just had to hope it was enough to see them through the season.

Saturday, 2 January 2016
Deepdale
EFL Championship
Preston North End 2 (Doyle 64', Clarke-Harris OG 90+4')
Rotherham United 1 (Andreu 35')

Rotherham kicked off the New Year with a trip to Preston North End, who were still finding their feet in the Championship since the two teams played out a goalless draw in August. The Millers' away form became a talking point after the game following a fourth straight defeat on the road. It was a run that would extend to one point in eight games away from home.

The Millers had their chances in the first half, but it was Norwich City loanee Tony Andreu who made it 1-0 with 35 minutes gone. The Frenchman started the move and finished it. But if Redfearn's New Year's resolution was for his side to defend their leads better, they failed at the first hurdle. They defended valiantly up until the equaliser, with both Paul Green and Joe Mattock producing goal-saving clearances. In the second half, Mattock was on hand to hook the ball off the line as the hosts protested that it had already crossed over, but referee Charles Breakspear wasn't having any of it.

Eoin Doyle – the striker for whom Rotherham reportedly tabled a bid in the region of £600,000 during the 2015 January transfer window when he was at Chesterfield – levelled for the hosts. The forward was scoring for fun for the Spireites in League One when he caught the eye of ex-Rotherham boss Evans but, after a move to Cardiff City didn't quite work out for the Irishman, he ended up at Preston.

With the momentum behind them, the Lancastrians pushed for a winner and with virtually the last kick of the game, they punished Rotherham. Marnick Vermijl's throw-in was headed on by Jonson Clarke-Harris, who diverted the ball into his own net to win it for the Lilywhites. The Millers went home empty-handed once again.

Manchester City loanee Facey was handed his professional debut, replacing experienced full-back Frazer Richardson, who picked up a concussion in the previous game against Fulham, and Facey's performance was one of the few things Redfearn was pleased with. What he wasn't so delighted with was the growing list of injuries as his players formed a queue outside the treatment room. Rawson picked up an injury during the game against Preston while Lee Frecklington's hamstring strain was expected to rule him out for around three weeks. Leon Best was due to have a groin operation and Stephen Kelly's knee would keep him out until March. The spate of injuries couldn't have come at a worse time.

Saturday, 9 January 2016
Elland Road
FA Cup
Leeds United 2 (Carayol 45', Doukara 90')
Rotherham United 0
The chance for a rematch presented itself to Steve Evans after his Leeds United side slipped to a 1-0 defeat to Rotherham back in November. After being drawn against the Whites in

the FA Cup third round in December, Rotherham's return to Elland Road less than two months on wasn't quite as enjoyable as the first time around. The moment came and went for Redfearn's men as the Whites booked their place in the fourth round with a 2-0 win over the Millers, who were dealt a third straight defeat in all competitions.

On his debut for the West Yorkshire side, Mustapha Carayol let Leeds fans know what he was about when he broke Rotherham's resistance on the stroke of half-time with a screamer. The lesser-spotted Emmanuel Ledesma made an appearance off the bench – his first sighting since a 2-1 defeat to Brentford in Redfearn's first game in charge in October. He replaced Danny Ward in the 57th minute but made little impact.

The Millers conceded a second late in the day in what was described as a 'comical' goal. Marco Silvestri's goal kick bounced all the way through but Rotherham stopper Lee Camp and defender Richardson – a Leeds United academy graduate – got their wires crossed. Richardson left it for Camp but Souleymane Doukara was determined to chase it down and he got his reward when he swiped the ball from right under the keeper's nose and slotted home to make it 2-0.

Evans had got one over Rotherham, who were now out of all cup competitions. As the saying goes, Redfearn's side could now use all of their energy to focus on the league. And if you'd asked any Millers supporter, the three points they'd taken from Leeds in the league back in November were far more important than a cup run.

Tuesday, 12 January 2016
New York Stadium
EFL Championship
Rotherham United 2 (D. Ward 45', Derbyshire 86')
Brighton & Hove Albion 0

Brighton & Hove Albion hadn't lost a game on their travels in the league when they made the long trip up to South Yorkshire. Be that as it may, Chris Hughton's side – who finished the season in third – were without a win in their last seven outings in all competitions and defeat against the Millers extended a four-game losing streak. For Rotherham, it was the reverse. Despite losing three games on the bounce, the Millers didn't have a bad record on home soil of late and victory against the Seagulls made it four wins in five at the New York Stadium.

In the end, Redfearn's side were well worth the 2-0 win they came away with. Right on half-time, Danny Ward volleyed the ball into the bottom corner at David Stockdale's near post to make it 1-0 to the hosts.

A second eventually came in the 86th minute when Derbyshire produced a neat finish to flick the ball into the top corner with the outside of his boot. It was a result that moved Redfearn's men up to 20th in the league on a 'perfect night', giving Rotherham a bit of breathing room while buying the boss some more time.

'I really enjoyed playing under Redfearn,' remarks Grant Ward. 'We tried to change the philosophy a bit. We played some really good football, but we just weren't getting the results. Sometimes, if you come in during the middle of the season when he did, it's a bit risky. If he had a full pre-season and started the season, I think it would've worked. We tried to play nice, expansive football on the floor and if we made a mistake, we got countered on and teams set up to do that.'

Saturday, 16 January 2016
New York Stadium
EFL Championship
Rotherham United 0
Queens Park Rangers 3 (Hoilett 52', Phillips 54', Polter 90+1')

The New York Stadium had football royalty in attendance when the Millers entertained the Hoops. Ex-Queens Park Rangers boss Neil Warnock paid a visit to his homeland to enjoy the hospitality and take in a meeting between two of his former clubs. Warnock's last spell in a hotseat came at Loftus Road when he stepped in as caretaker for a second spell in charge of the club in November 2015 following the dismissal of Chris Ramsey. Having won the Championship title in 2010/11 with QPR to end their 15-year exile from the Premier League, the Londoners turned to someone they could trust but after his temporary stint with the club came to an end, Warnock hadn't been spotted in a dugout since.

Warnock, who played for Rotherham between 1969 and 1971, had seemingly ruled out a full-time return to the profession while in charge of QPR before the club confirmed the appointment of Ramsey's successor, Burton Albion's Jimmy Floyd Hasselbaink. He could sit back and relax when he came to South Yorkshire to watch the game, but little did he know that just under a month later, he'd be watching on from the dugout rather than the dining hall.

The Millers were in search of a fourth consecutive home win and the first half demonstrated why Rotherham had performed considerably better at home of late. They could have been 3-0 up themselves at half-time but the simple fact was that they weren't.

Despite selling star striker Charlie Austin to Premier League side Southampton hours before kick-off, QPR still had options. Less than ten minutes into the second period, the visitors went ahead through Junior Hoilett and, just two minutes later, the Hoops doubled their advantage through Matt Phillips. The Millers looked all out of fight and it made it only too easy for Sebastian Polter to breach Rotherham's defence and make it 3-0.

On the back of that performance, there was no doubt that Warnock would have made some mental notes on the players he was going to get acquainted with very soon. Once he did become Rotherham boss, he couldn't say he didn't know what he was letting himself in for.

Saturday, 23 January 2016
Cardiff City Stadium
EFL Championship
Cardiff City 2 (Pilkington 25', 60')
Rotherham United 2 (Newell 44', Pilkington OG 49')
It was disheartening – not to mention worrying – that Rotherham could put in a dominant display like they had in the first half last time out against QPR and have nothing to show for it. Redfearn's side were capable on their day but a 3-0 defeat to mid-table QPR wouldn't have caused many outsiders to bat an eyelid, even if the scoreline didn't tell the full story.

Ahead of Rotherham's visit to the Welsh capital to face Cardiff City, the pitch had been relaid after their own players and manager Russell Slade criticised the condition of the surface. Meanwhile, there was no place in the home club's matchday squad for former Millers striker Alex Revell – who Redfearn had expressed an interest in re-signing – with the striker eventually completing a move to MK Dons.

Anthony Pilkington opened the scoring for Cardiff but, somehow, the Millers found a way back into the game through Newell. Danny Ward's no-look ball over the top was inch perfect for Newell, who managed to find the bottom corner just minutes before the half-time whistle sounded.

The Millers led for the first time in the 49th minute. Pilkington grabbed his second goal of the game, but this time at the wrong end of the pitch as the Republic of Ireland international turned the ball into his own net. Nevertheless, he made up for his blunder when he equalised for the Bluebirds on the hour mark. Cardiff defender Lee Peltier – Rotherham's future co-caretaker manager – was sent off after putting in what Redfearn described as a potentially leg-breaking challenge and the game finished all-square. A point was better than nothing. It kept Rotherham out of the relegation zone and with two huge games on the horizon, it was crunch time.

Saturday, 30 January 2016
New York Stadium
EFL Championship
Rotherham United 1 (Burke 11')
Charlton Athletic 4 (Makienok 4', 69', Vetokele 44', Lookman 90+4')
Woeful, shocking, embarrassing. Just a sample of some of the language used by Rotherham fans to describe what came next as they took to social media to vent their frustrations. The Millers were within their rights to think they had a good chance to get something out of the game against Charlton Athletic. This was the type of team they were targeting, after all, as opposed to the league's big hitters.

Charlton were on to their third manager of the season in José Riga. The Belgian, who had been reappointed as the club's head coach earlier in January, had pulled off a similar survival mission back in 2013/14. With the south Londoners sitting fourth from bottom of the Championship by mid-March, the former Standard Liege boss steered the ship to safety.

Ahead of the clash, Charlton were winless in their last 11 league games and 12 in all competitions. Going into the game, a four-point gap separated the two teams, with Rotherham in 20th and Charlton second from bottom, but it seemed that the Londoners were the only team that showed up. The Millers, on the other hand, looked listless. They had underestimated the Addicks and it was a costly mistake.

Within four minutes, Simon Makienok fired Charlton into the lead and the Dane made it look easy, as was becoming a recurring theme. Thankfully, with 11 minutes gone, Burke had the Millers back on terms, netting his first goal since joining on loan from Nottingham Forest in the January transfer window. The Millers were hoping to get to half-time with the scores still level when Igor Vetokele made it 2-1.

In the second half, Makienok bagged his second of the afternoon when he headed home from Jóhann Berg Guðmundsson's corner in the 69th minute to make it 3-1. Clarke-Harris was presented with a chance to get Rotherham right back in it when the forward won a penalty after being hauled over by Charlton's Jorge Teixeira. However, he blazed the spot kick over the bar and the Addicks restored their three-goal lead in added time. Substitute Ademola Lookman made it 4-1 in the 94th minute to add insult to injury.

Points were at a premium for Rotherham. Charlton were on their trail, a single point now all that stood between the two teams. The next outing was a must-win for Redfearn's side, not least because it was a trip to rock-bottom relegation rivals Bolton Wanderers. Nobody needed reminding of the enormity of the situation now.

Saturday, 6 February 2016
Macron Stadium
EFL Championship
Bolton Wanderers 2 (Spearing 2', Woolery 90+2')
Rotherham United 1 (Burke 43')
For the first time since lifting themselves out of the bottom three with a 4-0 win over Bolton on Boxing Day, Rotherham – who finished the day in 22nd place – slipped back into the drop zone with defeat in the reverse fixture against Wanderers, who moved off the foot of the table for the first time since November. The Trotters – like Charlton – were gaining on them. Two must-win games had ended in two defeats.

Having been recalled from his loan spell at Chesterfield at the end of December – during which time he made five appearances for the Spireites in League One – Richard Wood came back into the side and he was thrown in at the deep end when Redfearn named the defender in the starting XI. It was a moment he had been dreaming about, quite literally. The night before the game, in his subconscious state, Wood dreamt that he found the back of the net in the game against Bolton, scoring in his sleep.

He remembers: 'I jumped up for a header and shouted my name and then I was red hot as well, so I said "I'm sweating!" As soon as I did that, I laid down and went back to sleep again. I was pleased to be back and it was a big game for me and I wanted to do well, so it was obviously on my mind.

'I've always slept-walked. I don't know if it's because I can't switch off properly, but I'd be doing all sorts of different things. I'd be jumping up to try and head a ball and trying to play football. I've done other stuff as well. I've baked cakes, not downstairs in the kitchen, but sat up in bed pretending to mix a cake. People aren't keen on me as a room-mate when we travel away. They've woken up in the night and I've been stood over the top of them, which is a scary thing, I suppose!

'Up to that point, it hadn't been great for me personally. I'd been out on loan a couple of times and not been involved with Rotherham at all. That was my first game of the season for Rotherham. He [Neil Redfearn] had kept an eye on me and I finally got recalled. I was trying to do as well as I could to get called back.'

Within 65 seconds, Wanderers were ahead through Jay Spearing. Brazilian winger Wellington Silva thought he'd doubled the Trotters' lead, only for the goal to be ruled out for offside. With half-time approaching, the Millers were back on level terms when Burke made it 1-1 with 43 minutes played. The hammer blow came deep into added time at the end of the game when Kaiyne Woolery scored his first goal in professional football and put a vital three points on the board for Bolton.

Redfearn believed his team were the better side on the day against Bolton but the table suggested otherwise. It prompted questions about what had happened to the team that had so effortlessly swatted aside Bolton on Boxing Day. Unavoidably, there were calls for a change and they were very much seen and heard.

League table:

Position	*Club*	*Pl*	*GD*	*Pts*
20	Bristol City	30	-22	28
21	MK Dons	29	-18	27
22	Rotherham United	30	-19	25
23	Bolton Wanderers	30	-21	24
24	Charlton Athletic	30	-30	24

As a new week rolled around, chairman Tony Stewart decided to take action. Of his 21 games in charge across a four-month period, Redfearn had lost 14 matches and the threat of relegation loomed large. Losing to the Trotters was the final nail in the coffin and desperate times called for desperate measures.

'It is with a heavy heart that we've parted company with Neil today,' a statement from the club read. 'As we all know, football is a results-driven business and, with 16 games to go, our aim has to be to retain our Championship status.

'Everyone at the club wishes Neil well with his future career and thanks him for his efforts and endeavour. Our focus now is 100 per cent behind appointing a first-team manager as soon as possible.'

There was a genuine feeling of disappointment – especially from the players who had enjoyed trying something new under Redfearn's leadership – that it hadn't worked out between the two parties. However, at this stage in the season, there was no time to be sentimental.

'Bolton were struggling as well, so that was a big game down at the bottom for us,' Newell recalls. 'He [Redfearn] didn't really get long enough in charge, but that's how ruthless the industry is. There's so much money at stake to stay in that league. The way that Redfearn wanted to play and the way he was as a guy and as a manager, I did feel sorry for him. It was a shame.

'The league is full of massive teams with massive fanbases. The infrastructure at a lot of clubs now because they've been in the Premier League at some stage means, financially, teams like Rotherham are always going to be up against it.'

While the club started the search for a new manager, Redfearn's assistant Nicky Eaden took charge of first-team matters, aided by fitness coach Paul Warne and goalkeeping coach Andy Dibble. However, first-team and development coach Andy Hughes – who arrived in December from Bolton, having worked with Redfearn at Leeds – also departed alongside the outgoing Rotherham boss.

A number of names were bandied about in the days following Redfearn's sacking. One of the more interesting candidates linked with the vacancy was Northampton Town boss Chris Wilder. The former defender – who represented Rotherham between 1992 and 1996, making 158 appearances – had previously been linked with a move back to South Yorkshire to manage his old club after Steve Evans's exit and Sky Sports reported that he was in the frame once again.

After helping the Cobblers avoid relegation into non-league football, Wilder's side were on course for the League Two title. Ironically, he had also replaced Redfearn as Halifax Town's manager back in the early 2000s, but it wasn't to be for a second time and those reports soon faded into the background.

Rotherham weren't taking any chances with their next appointment. They had one last roll of the dice to get it right and who else do you turn to when you're fighting for your lives in the Championship?

Chapter Six

Back to Basics

THOSE DULCET Yorkshire tones almost instantly offset any feeling of panic that might have crept into the camp by the time Neil Warnock was officially unveiled as the new Rotherham United manager. The Sheffield-born boss was appointed on a short-term contract until the end of the campaign late one Thursday evening in February 2016. A warm greeting of 'Ayup' echoed around the room as the media convened in readiness to hear what Warnock had to say as he made his first appearance in front of the local press, clad in a red-and-black Puma-branded tracksuit sporting the Rotherham club crest.

It wasn't the ensemble he was used to wearing when he was lounging around his Cornwall home, where everyone wrongly assumed he had retreated in a well-deserved retirement. It had been 412 days since the then-67-year-old had taken to a dugout in a permanent capacity. As such, while he'd been enjoying a slower pace of life on the south coast, it took a lot to tempt Warnock back up to South Yorkshire.

'It's the 14th time I've retired and my 15th comeback,' he joked in his press conference. If nothing else, it was worth a chuckle and, above all else, Warnock liked to put smiles on faces.

Talks were said to have concluded fairly quickly after his name entered the frame. Nonetheless, there were plenty of things to consider for Warnock when pondering his next managerial move, such as factoring in the ten-hour-plus round trip from his base in Cornwall to the New York Stadium. But the number one consideration was that his wife, Sharon, was receiving treatment for breast cancer following her diagnosis in November 2015.

'Sharon was having chemotherapy down in Cornwall and I went with her one morning,' Warnock recounted in an interview with *The Offside Rule*. 'She was talking about me to the nurse and I was sat there reading the paper. I could hear her saying "He never frumps the cushions" and "He splashes everywhere when he washes the pots" and telling her how I get on her nerves.

'That morning, Rotherham's chairman, Tony Stewart, asked if I'd go and help them out for the last two-and-a-half months. I said "I'm sorry, I'd love to, but it's too far for me." I said to my wife "Listen, darling. Tony from Rotherham rang me, so I'll go there if you want me to get out of your way." She said "Go on then, get off!"'

At a later date, when Warnock penned his programme notes for Rotherham's final home game of the campaign against Blackburn Rovers, he cast his mind back to the club's 3-0 defeat to QPR midway through January when he was in attendance at the New York. He credited the supporters as being one of the main reasons he took up the role after his wife Sharon gave him her blessing to have 'one last season in football'.

'When I came up as a guest to watch the game against Queens Park Rangers, I was absolutely overwhelmed with the reception I received and it went a long way to persuading me to take up the reins when I was approached,' he said in the matchday programme.

So, it transpired that his unofficial retirement from football management was little more than a sabbatical. Rotherham were dangling dangerously. The Millers occupied

22nd place when Warnock took to the hotseat, three points adrift of fourth-bottom Bristol City and only a point clear of Bolton Wanderers and Charlton Athletic in the bottom two. But it was about to get a whole lot worse.

One win in their last seven league outings and an unenviable run-in had already seen almost everyone write off Rotherham and had Warnock listened to them, the Millers would have been preparing for a season in League One. That was never going to be the case, though. A glance at his CV told the players and fans alike all they needed to know – not that there were many people around the club that didn't instantly sit up and take notice at the mere mention of his name.

His reputation preceded him and Rotherham were about to find out why. Warnock's pedigree spoke for itself, having won seven promotions in total – which later became a record eighth – with Scarborough, Notts County, Huddersfield Town, Plymouth Argyle, Sheffield United and Queens Park Rangers. But Rotherham were not looking to ascend; they were in a scrap at the wrong end of the table.

However, he was no stranger to the underdog ticket. Scarborough were favourites to finish bottom of the pile when Warnock managed the club, but he shook off the stigma. He helped Scarborough to reach the promised land of the Football League after delivering the Conference title in his first – and one of his fondest – promotion campaigns. But it was his efforts to keep Torquay United in the Football League back in 1993 that was most likely to inspire Millers fans who were wondering if he could repeat that feat and keep them in the Championship. Even Warnock's promotion teams were usually up against it. When he helped QPR out of the second tier for the first time in 15 years, there were plenty of other teams with bigger budgets and better players, but what they didn't have was Neil Warnock.

The Championship, which Warnock once pronounced as the toughest league in Europe, was a level he knew inside out. During his eight years managing his boyhood club Sheffield United, Warnock won promotion to the top flight in 2005/06. It was at Bramall Lane that he yielded some of his most famous dressing-room rants and that would resonate with Millers fans who, as far as they were concerned, recognised that their players needed reprimanding for the below-par performances they were putting in on a weekly basis.

Indeed, he hadn't lost his penchant for the game. It was quite the opposite. He was ready and raring to go, and the news of his appointment was met with a largely positive response. He was joined by his trusty sidekick, Kevin Blackwell, and there was a feeling that there was no better duo for the job.

However, what he was met with on his first day at the office was a despondent group of players devoid of any sense of direction. Scottish defender Kirk Broadfoot was not alone in thinking the club's fate was all but signed, sealed and delivered, and therein lay the problem.

'I thought we were gone,' Broadfoot says, matter-of-factly. 'When the manager came in, in his first meeting, he was quite a funny guy. He was like, "What am I doing here? Have you seen our fixtures? We've got no chance of staying up!"'

Rotherham still had five of the top six left to play in their final 16 games of the 2015/16 season. That included the top three at the time – Middlesbrough, Hull City and Burnley – along with a handful of other high-flyers still vying for a play-off spot – Sheffield Wednesday, Derby County, Ipswich Town and Birmingham City.

Nevertheless, if there was one thing Warnock possessed in abundance it was personality – something he was looking to inject back into the place. His man-management skills were second to none and if anyone's colourful character could bring a club back from the brink, it was his.

With that schedule playing on everybody's minds, Warnock rallied the troops at Rotherham's Roundwood training facility to make his introductions to the players he would be joining in the trenches for the foreseeable. He made no bones about the situation, according to skipper Lee Frecklington, and it didn't take long for the players he had at his disposal to buy into a new philosophy of stripping everything back to basics.

'I'll never forget when he came in. One of the first things he said to us changed our mindset immediately,' Frecklington notes. 'He sat us in the room at the training camp and he said, "Everybody outside this room thinks that you're relegated – little old Rotherham's going to be relegated – and the chances are we probably are, but let's have a good time and let's try and take all the pressure off." We looked at it in a different way after that.'

It wasn't the first time he'd helped Rotherham through a rough patch, either. Back in 2006, when Millers fans were appealing for funds to keep their club afloat, Warnock's Sheffield United made a donation to Rotherham's cause. The neighbouring Blades even paid the wages of Stephen Quinn and Jonathan Forte during their loan spells with Rotherham at the tail end of the 2005/06 season to ease the club's troubles.

But Warnock's association with the club goes back much further than that. In 1969, a fresh-faced Warnock signed for Rotherham from Division Four club Chesterfield as a player. The club held a certain appeal for Warnock, who was handed his debut by boss Jimmy McAnearney off the bench in a 2-0 win over Walsall in September that same year. Warnock finished up with five goals in 52 appearances in all competitions for Rotherham, providing service out on the wing to the likes of future England international Dave Watson.

In his 2008 autobiography, *Made in Sheffield*, Warnock recalled how, when he first arrived at Millmoor as a 20-year-old making his way in the world of professional football, the feeling of catching the attention of Third Division Rotherham was like 'winning the pools'.

This time, however, it was quite the opposite. This time, the odds were stacked against him.

* * *

Naturally, Warnock's first order of business when he arrived at the club was to take stock of his resources. Goalkeeper Lee Camp possessed more than a few redeeming qualities playing in a Rotherham side that couldn't buy a win. The 31-year-old was being kept busy on a regular basis and his performances would eventually earn him the club's player of the season award. It was one less selection headache for the boss.

'The one thing about the squad at the time was it was a big squad and the club carried a lot of professional players,' Camp explains. 'There was a lot of muchness of muchness, really. You could toss a coin for certain positions to decide who would play because nobody was really going to improve certain positions.

'That was the reality that Neil Warnock found when he came in, so he had to work through what he had and find out who were his best 20-odd players moving forward. He sort of built a mini-squad out of the squad we had and that took him ten days to two weeks to find that platform.'

It came as little surprise when Warnock approached one of his old favourites, out-of-contract Paddy Kenny, to sign the stopper for a fifth time in his career. Aged 37, Kenny loaned his expertise to the goalkeeping department, led by coach Andy Dibble. The former Premier League gloveman spent the remainder of the campaign waiting in the wings as back-up to Camp during his short stay at the club, with the up-and-coming Alex Cairns – signed by Neil Redfearn in January from Chesterfield – the only other option between the sticks.

The additions of attacker Jerome Thomas, who had most recently been on the books at Crystal Palace, and defender Lloyd Doyley, who brought to the table over 400 appearances for Watford in both the Premier League and the Championship, suggested Warnock was building a team of know-how.

'I always remember his first-ever meeting,' Joe Newell reminisces. 'Just before training started, it was on the grass, and we had Lloyd Doyley and Paddy Kenny join us. As soon as Paddy joined us, it was like, "Neil Warnock. Paddy Kenny. Standard." They joined us and the gaffer got us all in a circle and it was their first day.

'He went, "Right, lads. I'd just like to welcome Paddy and Lloyd to the club. I owe Lloyd some money and I play golf with Paddy every Thursday, so I thought they'd come in and help us out." We all laughed and he had a dead straight face. To this day, I still don't know if he was joking or being serious!

'He just had that aura about him. We got one result and then that gives you a bit of confidence. We were like, "You know what, we've got Neil Warnock in charge of us here. We're definitely going to stay up." This guy had done it his whole career.'

With the transfer window having already closed, Warnock was going to have to make the most of the squad he had, bar a handful of free agents. Luckily, what he saw was the opportunity to mould those players, who had already been written off by most, into virtually new signings. And if any player exemplified just how much of an impact Warnock had on the team, it was Greg Halford.

Halford had headed out on loan to Championship rivals Birmingham City in November, having fallen out of favour. The situation escalated and there didn't appear to be any coming back for the summer signing. He had become something of an outcast since his return, describing how his exile meant steering clear of Rotherham's training ground and instead getting minutes in with the youth team.

'I was dismissed to the under-23s,' he recalls. 'I wasn't allowed anywhere near the training ground and I wasn't allowed to have lunch and had to wash my own kit. I was literally exiled.'

He wasn't convinced his personal situation would improve under Warnock, either. Halford expressed concerns about his decision to rebuff the manager's advances when he was coming through the ranks at Colchester United. Warnock submitted a six-figure bid for the Essex club's shining starlet in the summer of 2006 but Halford decided against joining him at Bramall Lane.

'It was mixed emotions when he got appointed as manager,' Halford says. 'Earlier in my career, when I was 20 or 21 at Colchester, he was Sheffield United boss and he put in an offer for me which got accepted and I turned it down without even speaking to him. We'd played them earlier in the season and I disliked the way he spoke after the game and it was something I regretted ever since.

'I was a bit fearful of him coming in, but luckily enough for me, I had his assistant, Kevin Blackwell, as a manager [at Sheffield United in 2008/09], so he was a massive ally. I had that apprehensive thought in my head of, "Which way is this going to go?" The lads gave me the nickname "son of", which sort of stuck because I followed him to Cardiff as well the summer following.'

He needn't have worried. The transition was a smooth one for Halford, who turned the page and wrote himself into the story as one of the protagonists in Rotherham's bid for survival, featuring in all but one of the final fixtures under the new boss. And he enjoyed working under Warnock so much that he would later join him at Cardiff for a final promotion charge, along with striker Danny Ward, where they made further history together.

'I had a week or so back with the under-23s and when Birmingham said they couldn't do anything for a contract, I walked out of the manager's office and nearly started crying. I ended up coming back – that was an emergency loan for a month and I played four games there – then Warnock came in and brought me back from the dead.

'I had one training session and his first game was against Birmingham and we ended up drawing. He brought me on as a right midfielder because that's where I played for Kevin [Blackwell] at Sheffield United. It was like a new lease of life for me. I had my excitement back.'

Another player whose Rotherham career Warnock resurrected was Richard Wood. Since returning from a loan spell at Chesterfield, he played 90 minutes under Neil Redfearn against Bolton in the final game of his ill-fated reign before the ex-Leeds boss was dismissed. But the central defender knew he was likely to be in the new Millers manager's plans.

He recalls: 'When it got announced that Neil Warnock was getting the job, I knew that I'd be playing even before I'd met him and gone into training that next day. I knew what he was about and I knew I was his sort of player. I've played against his teams loads of times, so I knew he liked me from previous Sheffield United–Sheffield Wednesday games.'

He was another player with a point to prove and a new manager to impress ahead of Warnock's first game in charge against Birmingham City, which came just two days after his unveiling. He had 16 games left to save Rotherham's season, but could they pull it off?

Saturday, 13 February 2016
New York Stadium
EFL Championship
Rotherham United 0
Birmingham City 0

Warnock insisted that he wanted to get to work immediately after accepting Stewart's offer to become the new Rotherham boss. If he was doing a job, he was doing it properly and he needed all the time he could get with his new group of players ahead of his first game at home to Birmingham.

He told the club's official website: 'When I spoke to the chairman on Thursday night, I think he was a bit surprised when we were talking about next week and I said "No I want to come up tonight when I've finished talking with you and take over tomorrow." I think it's important because it's an opportunity to get some points and I couldn't afford to miss out on that with only 16 games left.'

Halford's former loan club were first up as the Warnock era got under way and the player in question came back into the matchday squad as the boss named him on the bench when the Blues visited the New York Stadium. What's more, there were over 11,000 fans in attendance – the club's highest home crowd since the visit of Bolton on Boxing Day – to witness Warnock's homecoming.

Reduced to nine men following the dismissals of defensive duo Richard Wood and Joe Mattock, Warnock's men held on for a share of the spoils. Mattock was shown a yellow card for a late challenge and Wood joined him in referee Richard Clark's book in the second period. Wood saw red with ten minutes left on the watch after taking down Clayton Donaldson and it wasn't long before Mattock received his marching orders after failing to take a throw-in with enough haste in the Millers' own half. But instead of being scolded by his new gaffer, it earned him Warnock's plaudits.

Mattock reveals: 'Warnock said, "If we're winning, I want you to slow the game down." I got sent off because I'd been yellow-carded in the game and it was the 90th minute and I had a throw-in in the corner. I looked over and, as I'm walking down to get the ball, he's telling me to slow down but I'm already walking to the ball. When I got the ball in my hand, I couldn't quite take the throw-in and he's saying "Slow it down, slow it down".

'The next thing, the referee comes over to me, double yellows me and I get sent off. As I'm walking down the tunnel, he [Warnock] actually gives me a pat on the back because a minute later, the referee blows for full time. We got a point from it, but every point counts when you're in a relegation scrap.'

The boss dodged defeat in his opening fixture, having last lost his first game in charge of a club in 1997 when Oldham Athletic slipped to a 2-1 defeat against Bradford City after Warnock arrived in Greater Manchester in February the same year. The Latics would go on to be demoted to Division Two under Warnock, who saw his résumé tainted by a relegation. It was one of just a handful of blemishes on an otherwise outstanding CV, the others coming with Notts County in 1991/92, Bury in 1998/99 and Sheffield United in 2006/07.

It was a valuable point as the Millers began their efforts to stave off relegation under new management with a renewed sense of hope. Nobody expected Warnock's side to come out looking like a team reborn after just one or two training sessions – far from it – but it felt as though the wheels were in motion and, in light of recent results, a goalless draw against a top-half team was an improvement upon a thrashing at the hands of a relegation rival.

'Instead of complicating the style that we played, he just simplified everything,' Mattock continues. 'Free kicks next to the halfway line got pumped into the box and throw-ins were going down the line, and there was no playing out from the back – we were just putting pure pressure on the opposition. We almost became a super, well-drilled team where everyone knew their jobs and that's why we became so successful.'

Mattock was right, but Rotherham were still five points adrift as it stood. It would be up to Warnock and his players to turn those draws into wins and the boss had enough faith to go around for everybody. After the game, he asserted that he believed his team could 'compete with anyone at the moment'.

He declared: 'I said to the lads that it's only one game gone. Imagine what you can do in the next 15. It's exciting times.' As well as first-rate man-management skills, an infectious passion for the game and a tenacious will to win, anyone might have thought Warnock had added psychic powers to his growing list of personal qualities.

Saturday, 20 February 2016
Turf Moor
EFL Championship
Burnley 2 (Vokes 27', Arfield 86')
Rotherham United 0

That sinking feeling which Rotherham fans had become familiar with soon threatened to return and snuff out that flash of hope. Consecutive defeats against Burnley and Reading followed the Birmingham stalemate as Warnock waited patiently for his first win.

Champions elect Burnley were looking to extend their eight-game unbeaten run in the league and it became nine after seeing off Warnock's side. Goals from Sam Vokes and Scott Arfield either side of the break saw to that as the Clarets closed the gap on the table-topping Tigers while Rotherham were unmoved in 22nd place. Debutant Lloyd Doyley brought down George Boyd inside the penalty area, teeing up Vokes to convert the resulting penalty. The Millers registered just one shot on target in 90 minutes, but they didn't give up without a fight. In the 79th minute, an opening presented itself to Joe Newell and the travelling fans had faith in the winger to rescue a point for the visitors.

'We were 1-0 down with five or ten minutes to go and I got put through one-on-one with the keeper and I put it wide when I should've scored,' Newell explains. 'That was the only real clear-cut chance and if I'd scored, we might've nicked a point there. He didn't give me a bollocking or anything, but he kind of said "Listen, son, I know you've not meant to, but if that chance goes in, it might've been different".'

Arfield made it 2-0 to kill off the game just minutes later and the defeat signalled the end of Newell featuring in Warnock's starting line-up.

He remembers: 'The next week before the next game, he pulled me in and was like, "Joe, listen. If I came in at the start of the season, I love you as a player and I love your left foot … you'd be playing for me every week. However, I'm basically telling you now that you're not going to start another game for me this season. I need to go 4-5-1 and we're going to be really hard to beat. It's just not suited for you for how I'm going to play."

'But he said, "I still need you. You're going to come on every game and be my first sub, so don't be too down." Nobody wants to hear it but, at the same time, if a manager is honest with you, you can't really moan. True to his word, he didn't start me again.'

'He knew what he wanted, and he knew he wanted experienced players in the team that could achieve the job which got done in the end,' Clarke-Harris, another player who would be reduced to the odd cameo off the bench, adds. 'It makes complete sense and he got the job done in the end, which was all that mattered. You have to give him full credit for that. Until the last ball is kicked on the final day and anything is confirmed, you still have to give yourself the best fighting chance.'

Warnock remained upbeat and didn't let the result dampen his spirits. Burnley would go undefeated for the remainder of the season as Sean Dyche's men secured the title. Warnock had 'no complaints whatsoever' with his side's application and he couldn't fault his players, in spite of the outcome.

Tuesday, 23 February 2016
Madejski Stadium
EFL Championship
Reading 1 (Robson-Kanu 66')
Rotherham United 0

A midweek defeat at the Madejski Stadium left Warnock questioning for the first time since taking charge whether he was cut out for the drama of a relegation scrap. It was as if normal service had resumed for Rotherham. He could be heard muttering under his breath 'I'm getting too old for this' after his team reached their lowest ebb. The setback was, by his own admission, taking its toll on the boss.

Mattock and Wood returned to the starting line-up after serving their individual suspensions, but Rotherham were without Danny Ward after the forward suffered a concussion against Burnley. Hal Robson-Kanu scored the only goal of the game for Reading, opening his Championship account for the season as the Royals secured their first victory in six league outings. Elsewhere, MK Dons picked up a point at home to Huddersfield Town in a 1-1 draw.

Historically, the Millers' encounters with Reading have tended to materialise as key dates in the calendar. Later in October that year, the following season, Kenny Jackett's Rotherham would also be on the losing end of a 1-0 scoreline against the Royals. And in February 2019, it was a certified six-pointer with the two teams – Reading in 21st and Rotherham in 22nd – separated only by goal difference going into the clash. But Warnock, who said it was 'not for the lack of trying' from his players in the game, was not one to call it quits so easily.

'We have just got to keep going' was the message from the boss – not that they had much choice in the matter. They say it gets worse before it gets better, but it was difficult to resonate with that sentiment that particular evening. It was pointed out that, after losing game number 21 of the season, only Warwickshire-based non-league outfit Bedworth United – who played in the seventh tier at the time – had lost more games than Rotherham. The gap between Rotherham and MK Dons opened up to six points. If you had to put your money on one team of the bottom four to dodge the drop, it would have been the Buckinghamshire club. As it stood, it was out of Rotherham's hands.

'You cling on to hope, but the way we were playing – we were leaking goals and we weren't scoring goals – it seemed really bleak,' Halford says. 'We were favourites to go down with the bookies and all the fans of other clubs. Nobody could anticipate what Neil would come in and do. He got us enjoying football again, which was a major thing. Everyone was coming into training with a smile on their face. That turnaround, I don't think we're likely to see that again in our lifetime in that division. It's still very close to my heart.'

League table:

Position	*Club*	*Pl*	*GD*	*Pts*
20	Bristol City	33	-23	34
21	MK Dons	33	-19	32
22	Rotherham United	33	-22	26
23	Bolton Wanderers	33	-23	25
24	Charlton Athletic	33	-34	25

Away from the events unfolding on the pitch, the mood had picked up in the wake of Warnock's arrival. So, it was back to the training ground to see if the boss could salvage Rotherham's season. And it wasn't quite as doom and gloom as things might have appeared from the outside looking in.

'He made people accountable and got people doing their jobs,' Camp highlights. 'He made clear what he expected in no uncertain terms. It was challenging at times because of the expectation he has of you and the levels and standard he wants to achieve. At the same time, people thrived in that. Players wanted to be challenged and they wanted to be tested.

'His man-management is second to none. He was probably what we needed – without any disrespect to Neil Redfearn – because he was a completely different character and his way of doing things was there for all to see.'

Behind the scenes, there was somebody else who deserved just as much credit as the manager himself. Warnock's number two, Blackwell, was never far behind him – they came as a package deal. It was a bond over three decades in the making. Warnock first came across Blackwell when he signed the former goalkeeper for Scarborough in 1986 from non-league Barnet. The stopper grasped the opportunity with both hands as the Seadogs won promotion to the Football League under Warnock's tutelage. Warnock signed Blackwell a second time for Notts County in 1993 before the pair reunited once again at Torquay in Paddy Kenny-esque fashion.

Blackwell took his first steps into coaching when his superior made him player-assistant coach at Huddersfield before being named player-youth coach alongside Warnock at Plymouth Argyle. The pair linked up again at Bury when Blackwell took up the role of goalkeeping coach before making the transition to Warnock's number two – a title he carried over to Bramall Lane.

The Luton-born keeper went it alone for a period as he stepped out of Warnock's shadow but the two joined forces at Palace when Blackwell was named the club's technical director. And it seemed there was only one man fit for the job when Warnock chose his partner in crime to assist him in his latest role at Rotherham. Warnock and Blackwell picked up where they left off for one last hurrah, or so they mistakenly thought.

'We used to do all the structural work with Kevin Blackwell – who is a brilliant coach – during the Monday,

Tuesday and Wednesday,' Frecklington explains. 'Then Thursday and Friday, I remember training being so enjoyable. It was fun five-a-sides and Warnock would come out and tell stories and have a joke.'

First-team coach Ronnie Jepson made up the final member of the so-called 'Holy Trinity'. The former striker – for whom Warnock paid a five-figure fee to sign him for Huddersfield from Exeter during his playing days – joined up with the boss in a reserve-team coaching capacity at Crystal Palace in July 2009. Jepson, who won promotion with Warnock at Huddersfield as a player in 1994/95, remained with him at QPR and later Leeds. He went on to work with Blackwell at Bury before the trio came together at the New York Stadium. Their pasts, presents and futures were entwined.

'I remember him [Warnock] walking out on to the training pitch in February when it was freezing, and it must've been about zero degrees, but the sun was out,' Mattock recalls. 'He had on these massive Oakley glasses, just strolling down the side of the pitch while everyone is training.

'Blackie had his own ways as well. There were times where I used to think, "Do these two actually even like each other?" They always had the same principles, but they didn't let one another talk over each other. They'd always start bickering and we'd be stood on the pitch listening to it. We'd be like "Right, are we carrying on training or are you two having a row?" That's just passion for you. Both of them wanted to win and the players wanted to win.'

There were no egos to be found in the team, either. Warnock saw to that. Instead, his side would need to call upon that collective wisdom – along with Warnock's own 36 years in football management – as the players and staff put their heads together and their bodies on the line for the cause.

Former England under-21 international Matt Derbyshire spent a few years plying his trade in the top flight with

Blackburn Rovers in the early part of his career, while Leon Best also made his bow in the Premier League as a youngster with Southampton. Republic of Ireland international Stephen Kelly came through the ranks at Tottenham Hotspur, going on to play at the highest level with the likes of Birmingham and Fulham, making the cut for Euro 2012 as the Boys in Green qualified for that tournament for the first time since 1988.

Similarly, Halford had played in the top tier with Reading, Sunderland and Wolverhampton Wanderers. And Broadfoot had amassed over 100 appearances for European giants Rangers having been capped for Scotland a handful of times alongside his club career.

'When Warnock came in, he knew we needed to add a bit of experience, but we had a well-rounded team,' Derbyshire acknowledges. 'I played at the highest level and you can get lads that think they're this and think they're that but, being at that club, it was an amazing group to work with. When Leon came in, there was a lot of talk about him being this sort of character, but he was an absolutely fantastic boy to work with.'

Now, it was just about putting what they had learned on the training ground into practice. The 12-week project Warnock talked of was well under way and time was ticking. Fortunately, the games were coming thick and fast and, just five days later, Brentford would pay a visit to the New York Stadium. It would give the Millers a chance to get their roller-coaster ride of a season back on track and, more importantly, stop the rot.

There was little solace to be found in evaluating and re-evaluating the division's standings. All they could do was focus on their own results which, admittedly, is easier said than done. Anything above the bottom three would do. The fight to stay in the division was beginning to heat up and, as the Championship has proven time and again, just about anything can happen.

Bristol City were beginning to pull away from the fray, making it four wins in five league outings in February. The 20th-placed Robins were eight points clear of the Millers as the month drew to a close. It was shaping up to be a four-way scrap between Rotherham, MK Dons, Bolton Wanderers and Charlton Athletic.

'You've got to keep the faith. You can't ever think you're down and out,' Mattock says. 'When Warnock came in, it was a massive change. He was very no-nonsense. He said "Look, at the end of the day, my job is to keep you from getting relegated and that's what I'm going to do." Training changed and everything about the games changed.

'As soon as he came in, he was telling players what he thought of them, what he thought their traits are and what they're not good at. It's refreshing in a way because you get managers that beat around the bush with players. He's straight down the line and he knows what a player is good at.'

'I've never been a manager that picks a club for this or that and I've always picked challenges in my career,' Warnock said in one of his first interviews with the club after being announced as the new Rotherham boss. 'Usually, I'm trying to get a club promoted or get them in the play-offs, so it's a bit different.'

If a challenge was what Warnock wanted, then a challenge was what he had got. With 13 games remaining, a season-defining run was on the horizon and the almost unfathomable sequence of events that followed would go down in the club's history as one of the most memorable chapters in its 91-year existence.

The game that paved Rotherham's way back to the Championship at Wembley in the League One play-off final (Photo: Alamy)

Steve Evans dons a sombrero for the final game of the 2014/15 campaign at Elland Road (Photo: Alamy)

Neil Redfearn takes to the dugout at the New York Stadium for the first time against Reading (Photo: Alamy)

Neil Warnock is officially unveiled as the new Millers boss for the remainder of the 2015/16 season (Photo: Alamy)

Neil Warnock during his playing days at Rotherham United, taken in August 1971 (Photo: Colorsport)

Lee Camp celebrates against Brentford as Neil Warnock secures his first win as manager of the club (Photo: JR Brailsford)

Matt Derbyshire wheels away after scoring the winner in the South Yorkshire derby (Photo: JR Brailsford)

Neil Warnock celebrates victory over arch-rivals Sheffield Wednesday (Photo: JR Brailsford)

Kirk Broadfoot is relieved in the wake of victory over the Owls (Photo: JR Brailsford)

Leon Best scores to make it 2-3 against Derby County in a six-goal thriller at the New York Stadium (Photo: JR Brailsford)

The comeback is complete against the Rams as Rotherham rescue a late point (Photo: JR Brailsford)

Neil Warnock is overjoyed after his team keep the unbeaten streak alive against Derby (Photo: JR Brailsford)

Leon Best scores the only goal of the game in a 1-0 win against Ipswich Town (Photo: Trevor Price)

Neil Warnock has a smile on his face after Rotherham make it four wins in five by beating Ipswich (Photo: Trevor Price)

Lee Frecklington finds the back of the net against boyhood club Leeds United (Photo: JR Brailsford)

Neil Warnock along with coaching staff Kevin Blackwell and Ronnie Jepson are elated following the victory over Leeds (Photo: JR Brailsford)

Richie Smallwood takes aim from distance against MK Dons … (Photo: Trevor Price)

… and Richie Smallwood celebrates with his team-mates when his effort hits the back of the net (Photo: JR Brailsford)

Kirk Broadfoot makes the scoresheet against relegation rivals MK Dons (Photo: JR Brailsford)

Lee Camp salutes the supporters following a huge victory away at MK Dons to take a step closer to safety (Photo: Trevor Price)

Chapter Seven

The Unthinkable

THE 2015/16 season in English football was unprecedented for several reasons. Above all else, Leicester City monopolised the headlines. After just about managing to stay up in 2014/15 after pulling off a great escape of their own, Leicester – who were given 5,000/1 title odds at the beginning of the term – won the Premier League. They became just the sixth club to do so, the achievement confirmed on 2 May 2016 after Chelsea and Tottenham Hotspur drew 2-2 at Stamford Bridge. There were even rumours of Hollywood interest in making a movie based on Jamie Vardy's very own Roy of the Rovers memoirs.

Leicester took the title from Chelsea, whose season went horribly wrong from the opening day when José Mourinho clashed with club doctor Eva Carneiro after she entered the pitch to treat Eden Hazard in their game against Swansea City. She left her post shortly after amid the fallout from the highly publicised row and, in the summer of 2016, Carneiro's employment tribunal claim for constructive dismissal was eventually settled.

Elsewhere, Jürgen Klopp's appointment at Liverpool in October 2015 cannot be overlooked in the season's timeline. The German was named as the new Liverpool boss after Brendan Rodgers had his contract terminated in the wake of the Merseyside derby. Klopp – or 'the Normal One' as he dubbed himself on his arrival – had been managing Bundesliga club Borussia Dortmund before signing a three-year deal at Anfield, where he would leave a lasting legacy by the time he announced in January 2024 that he would be stepping down at the end of that season.

Meanwhile, Anthony Martial became football's most expensive teenager when he completed a £58m move to Manchester United from Monaco. The forward, who was tipped for big things, cost the Premier League giants a 'ridiculous amount of money' in Louis van Gaal's own words. The United boss justified the fee by explaining it was simply 'the crazy word we are in'. It was about to get even crazier in the lower leagues.

Saturday, 27 February 2016
New York Stadium
EFL Championship
Rotherham United 2 (Derbyshire 29', D. Ward 71')
Brentford 1 (Judge 43')

Given that Rotherham United's home attendance reached its season low when they entertained Brentford in late February, the players out on the pitch couldn't believe how the noise carried during the game. The club's supporters rallied behind their team in a match which marked the beginning of a record-equalling, season-salvaging unbeaten run. Bearing in mind how the last seven months had unfolded, you could hardly blame those fans that opted to follow the action from a distance in the comfort of their own homes, but those that were in the crowd were about to witness vintage Neil Warnock at his best.

The Football League's result of the day – as announced on social media – came from the New York Stadium. It was the start of something special – a Millers side revived under Warnock. Rotherham had conceded a total of ten goals in the opening 15 minutes of their matches, going behind first in

21 of their 34 league games, and Lee Camp had to be alert between the sticks early on.

The deadlock was broken on the half-hour mark by Matt Derbyshire, who scored the first goal of the Warnock era and his fifth of the campaign to put the Millers ahead. Lee Frecklington set up the club's leading marksman, who was perfectly placed to slot home the opener, lifting his shirt over his head in celebration to display a birthday message for his twin boys.

For a team in possession of the division's worst defensive record, Rotherham expected the worst when the man in the middle, Mark Brown, pointed to the spot with just minutes to go until half-time. Frecklington's challenge on Brentford winger Sergi Canos thwarted the Spaniard before he could pull the trigger, with Brown later admitting to Frecklington that he felt he had made the wrong call. Camp guessed correctly, diving down low to his right to keep out the penalty from Judge, but the Millers stopper wasn't quick enough to reach the rebound and the visitors levelled proceedings in the 43rd minute.

The introduction of Danny Ward in the second half of the game turned out to be a smart move. Having come close to seeing the net bulge moments before with a venomous volley which was tipped on to the bar by David Button, the substitute was on hand to help Rotherham restore their lead in the 71st minute. The ball squirmed under Button at his near post to make it 2-1 to the home team. However, they had to see out a tense final 15 minutes, with Kirk Broadfoot covering every inch of the pitch with his head tightly bandaged in a red gauze.

Camp saved from Millers old boy John Swift, who should have equalised for Brentford, before Frazer Richardson's goalline clearance from Philipp Hofmann allowed the New York Stadium to let out the breath it had been holding in for the latter stages of the game. When Lasse Vibe was put through on goal in the dying moments of the game, it could have spelled heartbreak for Rotherham had it not been for Camp once again getting down well.

The full-time whistle was music to the players' ears as it confirmed a timely first victory under Warnock. Meanwhile, both MK Dons and Charlton Athletic fell prey to late winners, with the Dons beaten 3-2 by Blackburn Rovers in added time, whilst the Addicks were overcome 4-3 by Reading. With Bolton Wanderers otherwise engaged in the FA Cup, the table was already looking a lot healthier for Rotherham, with the deficit between the Millers and MK Dons now halved to three points.

Even Brentford boss Dean Smith, who Rotherham had wanted to replace the outgoing Steve Evans earlier in the season before Smith took over at Brentford in November 2015, conceded the Millers deserved to take all three points. Warnock had finally found a winning formula and he was going to stick to it.

'When you look at the next few weeks, we have a South Yorkshire derby at Sheffield Wednesday followed by home games against Middlesbrough and Derby,' Warnock wrote in his matchday programme notes ahead of the game. 'I don't suppose the bookies will be giving us good odds, but this is when we really need to roll our sleeves up, go out, give it our all and enjoy the moment.'

Saturday, 5 March 2016
Hillsborough
EFL Championship
Sheffield Wednesday 0
Rotherham United 1 (Derbyshire 21')

Throngs of people dressed in both the red and white of Rotherham and the blue and white of Sheffield Wednesday eagerly awaited the arrival of the Millers' team bus at Hillsborough on Saturday, 5 March 2016. They were all hoping to catch a glimpse of one man and as soon as Warnock stepped off the coach, rivalries were reignited in South Yorkshire. The Rotherham manager hung back as his players disembarked the bus and made for the dressing rooms, allowing the crowd to simmer for a dramatic pause before he revealed himself like a pantomime villain. Warnock soaked up any jeering and booing from the opposition supporters like the showman he is, enjoying the theatre that came with the local match-up.

'That was the big one,' says former Owls defender Richard Wood. 'That's when we knew we were on to something. You always want to do well against your former clubs. It always happens where former players come and fans get riled by it, which just encourages it. Warnock loves going back to Hillsborough. He took the pressure off us lads because, even turning up, fans go mad and he gets all the stick.'

It's true that Rotherham fans generally consider Doncaster Rovers to be their nemesis – although it had been close to a decade since the two teams had gone head-to-head in a competitive fixture – whilst Wednesday's Steel City derby with Sheffield United is up there as one of English football's great rivalries. However, there is still something to be said for a Millers–Owls stand-off, especially as it was the closest either team were likely to get to a South Yorkshire derby any time soon, with Doncaster suffering relegation to League Two at the end of the season and Sheffield United finishing mid-table in League One.

It was Warnock's allegiance to the Blades, having been brought up as a boyhood Sheffield United supporter, that fuelled the fire. The Millers boss revealed in his pre-match press conference that he had been presented with 'three opportunities' to manage Sheffield Wednesday in the past, but despite the 'very tempting' offers, he turned down the Owls because of his loyalty to the Blades.

Warnock told the *Daily Mail* in an interview at the time: 'When our bus arrived at Hillsborough, there was a big crowd waiting for us and they were all pointing at me and shouting "W*****, w*****!" I told the lads to go to the dressing room and I stayed on for a while. I thought I'd make the Wednesdayites sweat a bit. Eventually, I got off and waved to them and said, "Thanks for waiting, everybody".'

As it happened, Warnock held an impressive record over the Owls, having presided over nine Steel City derbies during his time in the dugout at Bramall Lane. He recorded four wins and three draws, with the Blades most notably completing the double over their arch-rivals in 2005/06.

Rotherham, on the other hand, had failed to win any of their three previous encounters with the Owls since winning promotion back to the Championship. The Millers had slipped to a 2-1 defeat to Wednesday earlier in the season at the New York Stadium. The Owls had made Hillsborough a fortress, coming into the game unbeaten in their last 14 home league outings, with just two defeats in 22 games.

'It might be my last chance to manage a team at Hillsborough, so I am going to enjoy it,' Warnock told the club's official website in the build-up to the game. 'I think that South Yorkshire is the bedrock of football. People have told me about the London derbies and the ones in Scotland but, having been brought up in this area, for me, these derbies are the ones.'

All the signs were pointing towards an Owls win, but it was Rotherham who started the game on the front foot. Grant Ward had the chance to open the scoring early on but, with 21 minutes on the clock, Derbyshire was the man to draw first blood and make it 1-0 to the Millers. It all originated from Richardson's throw-in out on the right before Frecklington and Derbyshire combined once again to carve out the winner. Frecklington's ball into the box evaded everyone apart from Derbyshire, who was lurking at the far post to prod in the only goal of the game.

'Lee Frecklington played the ball across and I managed to get around the back post and tap it in,' Derbyshire recalls. 'There was a silence and chatter of "Oh my God, what's happening?" from their fans. That was a great result for us to go away, especially there, against massive rivals and get that win under the belt. It was amazing, not just for us but for the fans as well.'

Close to 29,000 supporters were packed into Hillsborough but it was the section of away fans housed in the Leppings Lane End who were in raptures when the striker broke the deadlock. Over the course of the two seasons he spent in South Yorkshire, it was almost indisputably Derbyshire's most memorable moment in a Rotherham shirt and earned him a place in the club's folklore. He was in esteemed company alongside the likes of Ben Pringle and Darren Garner, who were well known for rippling the net against the Owls.

For a long time, when the question 'Who put the ball in the Wednesday net?' was put to Rotherham fans, the answer was Scottish winger Joe McBride, who scored the winner against the Owls in December 1982. Then it was fast forward to February 2002 when Richie Barker stole the show with a stoppage-time winner over his former team – the club who gave him his start in football – in a 2-1 win for the Millers at Hillsborough.

For his part, Garner will forever be remembered for his wonder strike against Wednesday. Rotherham, whose opponents were in search of their first win of the 2002/03 campaign in the First Division at the time, had to come from behind away from home. Leading marksman Alan Lee levelled from the spot in the first half before Garner struck late in the day. Taking aim from 30 yards out, the substitute gave Owls keeper Kevin Pressman no chance as it finished 2-1 to Ronnie Moore's men in August 2002.

Meanwhile, Pringle's effort represented Rotherham in Mitre's 2013 goal of the year competition. It had been five long years since the two teams had locked horns when the Millers hosted the Owls in the first round of the 2013/14 League Cup. Ten minutes into the game – which was delayed to allow fans to filter into a New York Stadium which was close to capacity – Pringle had the Millers a goal to the good with a rasping strike which found the top corner and, after the Owls equalised, Frecklington made it 2-1 with an impressive effort of his own to cap off victory.

Whether it's Garner letting fly from distance to hold on to the bragging rights and wrap up all three points or Pringle winding up to take aim and fire Rotherham into the next round of the cup, there is a place reserved in the history books for the player who steps up when it matters most in a local derby.

For large parts of the game, it was one-way traffic and Rotherham had their backs to the wall to defend their slender lead. Aiden McGeady thought he'd levelled for the Owls but, after a lengthy delay, referee Chris Kavanagh came to the decision that the goal would be ruled out. McGeady's effort took a deflection off Owls defender Michael Turner – who was believed to be in an offside position by Kavanagh's assistant – on the way in. It was a let-off for the Millers. The Owls had a second goal chalked off after the break when Gary Hooper rippled the net, but it was a clear-cut call compared to the first incident. There was some debate after the game around the first disallowed goal, with Wednesday boss Carlos Carvalhal of the opinion that Turner was onside, but he couldn't deny that Rotherham had looked a solid outfit.

There was a lot riding on the game for both teams. Wednesday's play-off rivals, Cardiff City, had already done their bit and secured victory in the early kick-off, while Rotherham were running out of time to save themselves from the drop.

'The thing about playing at Hillsborough is once they get a bit of confidence, the crowd gets confident and it's a very loud – not hostile – atmosphere and you can hear everything,' Mattock – one of three ex-Owls who featured in the Millers' matchday squad along with Wood and Leon Best – explains. 'They were full of confidence and putting it on us, but we defended our lead really well. Every single player in the team worked their socks off.

'Matt Derbyshire was playing on the left in midfield next to me and we were pinned in for the last ten minutes. He was playing left wing-back and I was almost like a left centre-half, with five at the back. It was a really good shift. He played brilliantly and he was up and down all game.

'All the Sheffield Wednesday players were bombing forward. The full-backs were forward, the wingers were forward, the wingers were like strikers and the full-backs were like wingers.'

Derbyshire even requested that he trade in his shirt with his favourite number 27 on the back in favour of Mattock's number three jersey in recognition of the shift he put in on the left flank to see the game out as a makeshift full-back. It was only in the aftermath that the enormity of what he'd done – bagging the winner in the South Yorkshire derby – hit him.

'With the way we set up, we had the freedom to go and play, but we had bodies behind the ball and we were defending for our lives,' Derbyshire continues. 'I played on the left, on the right and everywhere, to be honest. Once we got our noses in front, it was about defending that lead and trying to get three points, because every point was humongous. At one point, I was playing at left-back.

'After the game, when we walked over to the fans and gave them a clap off, the atmosphere was electric. There are quite a few players at Rotherham before that had scored against Sheffield Wednesday, but I didn't realise until after the game what a big deal it was for the club and for the fans.

'The coaching staff made it known to us that we needed to stay in the Championship for our families, for the fans, for the club and for everything. It really sunk in and really helped us.'

Warnock's side had picked up three points on the road for the first time since beating Leeds United at Elland Road in November, putting a dent in Wednesday's promotion hopes in doing so. The Owls would go on to finish sixth and take the final play-off spot, eventually losing out to Hull City in the final at Wembley, while Rotherham's record at Hillsborough remained intact, unbeaten at the home of the Owls since 1981. They were also the first team to beat Sheffield Wednesday in their own backyard since Middlesbrough – who, ironically, were up next for Rotherham – in August. It was a win that was 'doubly enjoyable' for Warnock, whose phone was blowing up after the game with messages from fellow Blades fans.

Rotherham were brought back down to earth with the news that MK Dons had taken all three points from Queens Park Rangers, meaning Warnock's side were still three points adrift, but it couldn't take the shine off what had been an historic weekend for the Millers. They could enjoy it for now, but that result for MK Dons told them not to get too comfortable just yet.

Warnock had been called a lot of things during his career – some more complimentary than others – but Rotherham fans were so in awe of their new leader that they began to question if he was, in fact, the Messiah. Warnock was inclined to agree but added that if he was worthy of such a title, he was, in fact, 'the knackered Messiah'.

Tuesday, 8 March 2016
New York Stadium
EFL Championship
Rotherham United 1 (Frecklington 88')
Middlesbrough 0

A smash-and-grab in football is usually defined as a game in which a team – despite finding themselves up against it for the most part of the 90 minutes – manages to come away with all three points, whether they are deserving of them or not. And quite often, getting a result by digging deep and mustering up every last shred of grit and resolve is significantly more satisfying than a painless walk in the park. The result against Boro was battling, it was spirited and it was determined. It was everything you'd expect from a Rotherham United team and a Neil Warnock team, at that.

Just four months earlier, the Millers had accepted that the likes of automatic promotion-chasing Middlesbrough weren't the type of team that they could target for points. Such was the shift in attitude – helped by the back-to-back wins they had under their belt – that Rotherham were now plotting a way to win against a team who had one eye on the league title. Nevertheless, Warnock held Boro in high regard as 'the best side in the league', appreciating that his side were unable to 'compete with them in that respect'. In the end, the manager – who was named in the Football League's star XI of midweek alongside match-winner Frecklington – claimed that the victory was 'one of the best wins' of his career.

As for Rotherham fans, a win over local rivals Sheffield Wednesday seemed hard to eclipse, but when Middlesbrough came to the New York Stadium for a second Yorkshire derby in a week on a Tuesday evening in early March, it just about topped the victory over the Owls for different reasons. There was a chill in the night air – it was so cold that the players' breath was visible on the wind – but the Millers faithful were willing to brave the elements. If the Owls posed a tough test for Rotherham, then Boro would be the ultimate assessment. It remained to be seen whether Warnock's men could put Middlesbrough's league standing to their back of their minds for 90 minutes. Boro occupied second place, with league leaders Burnley just a point better off, and Aitor Karanka's side had every aspiration of catching up with the Clarets and making a late play for pole position.

'Around March time, we had Middlesbrough – my old club – and we had a pretty big run,' Richie Smallwood notes. 'I remember thinking, "Where are we getting our win from in here?" Middlesbrough were flying and Sheffield Wednesday were good at the time. The belief rocketed and those were the foundations that we built again.'

As the game kicked off, Rotherham experienced a let-off when David Nugent found himself one-on-one with Camp after getting the better of Richard Wood, who had a lapse in concentration at the back, only for Nugent to fire wide of the target. For large parts of the game, it was an onslaught. Gaston Ramirez rattled the post with a free kick and Nugent was unable to direct a header on target, blowing another glorious chance for Boro. Chances were few and far between for the Millers but when they did fashion an opening in the 88th minute, they profited from it.

Jonson Clarke-Harris used his strength to hold off Middlesbrough defender Dael Fry – another name Millers supporters might remember from his brief loan spell in South Yorkshire in 2016/17. The striker's delivery into the box was made for Frecklington, who arrived undetected to blast the ball into the roof of the net and make it 1-0 to the Millers. The midfielder threw himself into the perfect knee slide, gliding along the turf, which was slick from the downpour, reaching the corner flag where he was swamped by his team-mates, all while the rain continued to beat down on the New York Stadium.

'We were absolutely being battered for the whole match and I don't know how we were still in the game at 0-0, then the ball came to me on the edge of the box in the 88th minute,' Frecklington explains. 'We absolutely stole a win we should've never got.'

Moments later, Greg Halford was shown a second yellow card and sent down the tunnel and the Millers had to see out a shaky end to the game with ten men. Warnock had masterminded three consecutive wins in the second tier for the first time since December 2003 for the Millers.

'He just simplified things really and everyone knew their job,' Smallwood adds. 'He made us more solid in a 4-5-1, but we still had an attacking goal threat, a target man and a midfield that worked hard and was hard to break down. Everyone knew what they were doing. Once we got our set pieces sorted, which we worked on a lot, he had some brilliant ideas. A lot of teams in that division can't really handle it. I was fortunate enough to stay in his plans.'

It marked a turning point for a team who had been leaking goals earlier in the campaign. Not only had they made it two wins in as many games against high-flyers Sheffield Wednesday and Middlesbrough, but they were keeping clean sheets as well. Rotherham had managed successive shutouts on two previous occasions earlier in the campaign, against Leeds United and Bristol City in November, then Hull City and Bolton Wanderers in December. To replicate that, Warnock needed his players to revert to type; it was all a part of the Millers manager's survival masterplan.

Mattock recalls: 'I remember him telling me "Look, Joe, you're a typical young, attacking full-back but, for me, I need you to be a defender that stops crosses coming into the box and I need you to defend the goal, so stop thinking about going forward so much and defend with the back four." That was that, straight away, and that was my job.'

Fortune was beginning to smile upon Rotherham. MK Dons drew a blank with Charlton Athletic in a 0-0 draw at The Valley in a crunch six-pointer. Elsewhere, though, Bolton Wanderers ended a run of three straight defeats with a 2-2 draw against Ipswich Town.

'We got lucky a few times, but sometimes you make your own luck,' Wood says. 'From what we were ... we were dead and buried. Middlesbrough were flying at the time and they were up there. In the first half, they absolutely battered us and they had so many chances, I don't know how they didn't score. Everything just aligned for us to stay up. Everything we did, we couldn't go wrong – that's what it was.

'That was promotion form. Nobody wanted to come to Rotherham and play us and that's what you want – you want that fear. We played ugly. It didn't matter how we won as long as we won and we all knew that. It was dead simple and it paid off. Football is a simple game sometimes and it gets over-complicated.'

Rotherham's bodies-on-the-line performance demonstrated that, if nothing else, they were staging a fightback to be proud of. And if they needed any inspiration, they didn't have to look far from home. Rock bottom of League One midway through December, neighbouring Barnsley went on a late surge which lifted them out of the relegation zone and into the play-offs. The Reds would go on to achieve a Wembley double, beating Oxford United in the EFL Trophy Final and Millwall in the play-off final. The proof was in the pudding that it's never too late. In Warnock's own words, Rotherham had 'ten cup finals' left to play and, as he highlighted upon his arrival, just about anything can happen in the Championship.

'The Championship is my thing really,' said Warnock after the game. 'I love the blood and thunder.' He also revealed that keeping Rotherham in the division would be his best achievement 'by an absolute mile' if he could pull it off. He praised his side for 'fighting until the end', which would mirror the way they saw out the season.

'We are still in the bottom three after three wins, that shows how far away we were,' he said. 'Everybody knows we were dead and gone. We might still be dead and gone, but at least we've got a chance.'

League table:

Position	*Club*	*Pl*	*GD*	*Pts*
20	Bristol City	36	-25	37
21	MK Dons	36	-18	36
22	Rotherham United	36	-19	35
23	Charlton Athletic	36	-34	29
24	Bolton Wanderers	36	-25	26

Saturday, 12 March 2016
New York Stadium
EFL Championship
Rotherham United 3 (D. Ward 83', Best 85', 90+1')
Derby County 3 (Ince 55', 65', Martin 63')

As a matter of course, all good things must come to an end eventually. Often, when a team find themselves in a rich vein of form – such as the one the Millers were enjoying under Warnock – there comes a point when it feels almost too good to be true and the bubble is bound to burst at some stage. For Rotherham, Derby at home was the game that looked as though it would be their undoing in that respect, with Warnock himself admitting in his programme notes for the game against Middlesbrough that it 'doesn't come much tougher' than the Rams. It certainly looked as if Warnock's side had run out of steam by the time they found themselves trailing by three goals midway through the second half.

But there was to be a twist in the tale and by the time the full-time whistle came around, the Millers felt invincible. There was nobody Warnock's team wouldn't have given a run for their money.

The date – Saturday, 12 March 2016 – is one the majority of fans of the club would be hard-pressed to forget. It was the day when promoting-chasing Derby called in on the Millers. It is a fixture that will go down as one of the greatest games in the club's recent history – let alone the 2015/16 campaign as a standalone season – and one of the most entertaining games the New York Stadium has ever seen.

The games were coming thick and fast. Warnock's side had three consecutive wins behind them. Meanwhile, the Rams were looking to steady the ship and keep themselves in contention for a top-six finish. Derby boss Darren Wassall was appointed on an interim basis until the end of the season around the same time that Warnock arrived at Rotherham. The former Rams academy director took over from Paul Clement, who had been axed earlier in February. Wassall was to be mentored in his new temporary role by none other than Harry Redknapp, with Redknapp acting as a 'football advisor' alongside managing Jordan in the World Cup qualifiers.

One thing was for sure – if previous meetings between the Millers and the Rams were anything to go by, there wouldn't be any shortage of goals. In Rotherham's maiden season back in the Championship in February 2015, Steve Evans's side fumbled a 3-1 lead at the New York Stadium against Derby, eventually settling for a 3-3 draw, as Darren Bent levelled late on for the Rams. The roles were reversed just over 12 months on in an end-to-end encounter Warnock described as the 'result of the season'.

In the 55th minute, Tom Ince fired the Rams into the lead after some poor defending from Rotherham created an opening. Less than ten minutes later, Wassall's men doubled their advantage as Chris Martin made it 2-0 from close range. Almost instantly after the restart, the visitors capitalised on a mishap at the back to make it 3-0 as Ince claimed his second and Derby's third of the afternoon. There didn't appear to be a way back for Rotherham, who were less surprised and more disappointed to find themselves down and out, not for the first time. There were concerns that it could be a rout – maybe five or six for Derby – but there was a different quality to this Warnock side. Instead of waving the white flag and surrendering their hopes of keeping the unbeaten run alive with the kind of indifference that fans had come to expect from their team, they took matters into their own hands.

'We got told that we had to stand up and be counted and we did,' says Millers defender Mattock, who started the game.

With around 15 minutes left to play, the Derby supporters in the away end were chanting Wassall's name, but that was all about to change. A double substitution was on the way for the Millers. Warnock opted to replace experienced midfielder Paul Green with striker Leon Best and winger Joe Newell came on for Matt Derbyshire. The Rotherham boss was making a go of it.

'We came on at the same time,' Newell remembers. 'I came on thinking "Right, I just need to bring some energy and try and get on the ball. We're 3-0 down, so we're not going to get anything from the game. You know what, next week he might change his mind and he might start me."'

Derby made swaps of their own as goalscorer Martin and midfielder George Thorne made way for the Rams, who, not illogically at 3-0 up, thought they were cruising. But if one man was used to the taunts of the away supporters, it was Rotherham stopper Camp. The keeper came through the ranks at Pride Park with his hometown club before making the switch to the Rams' biggest rivals, Nottingham Forest, later in his career. And he was well positioned to hear the chants of the Derby fans behind his goal in the second period of the game.

'I always get stick when we play Derby, for obvious reasons,' Camp, who was with the Rams between 2002 and 2007, says. 'I remember standing there looking at the scoreboard and it was 13 or 14 minutes to go. It was 3-0, but I was thinking, "How is this a 3-0 game?" I thought it flattered them. They scored straight away from a short back-pass from Danny Collins from the kick-off – just something stupid that took the game out of sight for us.

'I never looked at it thinking, "We really deserve to be 3-0 down here." It was just weird. They'd gone from a 4-3-3 to a 4-4-2, which opened the game up. It just seemed to change within the substitutions and there seemed to be more space for us out wide to cross the ball.'

There was just seven minutes left on the watch when Danny Ward pulled a goal back for Rotherham. 'Merely a consolation, do we think?' asked the commentator after Grant Ward sliced open the Derby defence and Ward kept his composure to catch out keeper Scott Carson with a neat finish. Two minutes later, Newell's corner caused the Rams all sorts of problems. The set piece was glanced on by Derbyshire and substitute Best managed to bundle the ball over the line and hand the Millers a lifeline with 85 minutes gone. Time was ticking as Camp weighed up his options. He lofted the ball upfield in the hope that his team-mates could produce something out of the ordinary. Danny Ward got the ball down on the ground, lifted a cross into the box and the ball was met by the head of Best to make it 3-3 in the 91st minute. It was about as last-gasp as it gets. Even Leon Best didn't know which way to turn when the ball hit the back of the net. Everybody inside the stadium was gripped.

'You felt it all change,' Camp continues. 'Even though it was 3-1 with eight or nine minutes to go, you could feel on the pitch that Derby were completely unsettled and we had a shot of adrenaline. I could feel the Derby fans behind the goal were a bit nervous and all of a sudden thinking, "This isn't quite right."

'We were attacking the Rotherham end, so the fans were off their feet. You felt within five seconds of scoring the goal that the whole place changed. If the game had gone on another five minutes, we'd have won. It was one-way traffic. It was one of the craziest games I've been involved in.'

It wasn't the first time Leon Best had been involved in a game of that ilk, either. In February 2011, the striker was involved in the famous eight-goal thriller between Newcastle United and Arsenal. The Magpies – who were 4-0 down to the Gunners within 26 minutes of kick-off – scored four times in 19 minutes to snatch a point in a 4-4 draw, with Best netting Newcastle's second of the afternoon. The striker, who joined Rotherham on a deal until the end of the campaign in November 2015 following a successful trial period under former boss Neil Redfearn, played a starring role in the final run-in – not least by bagging the equaliser against Derby to secure one of the most important points of the season.

The former Republic of Ireland international managed four goals in 16 appearances during his fleeting stay in South Yorkshire, but they were four crucial goals in the Millers' season. For the man who had once commanded million-pound fees – with Blackburn Rovers, his last permanent club before Rotherham, parting with north of £3m to secure his services from Newcastle – it was a change of pace. The ex-Premier League goalscorer, who Warnock later said he wouldn't swap for any other Championship striker, explained that while the club's facilities were 'not a palace', there were few teams he'd been in that had the 'rare' team spirit the Millers possessed. Indeed, that was what gave Warnock's team the X-factor.

'Games like that just allowed us to believe in ourselves and have the confidence to get out of the position we were in. It was amazing really,' Danny Ward reminisces. 'It was late on, so you've got to keep going until the final whistle. When the second goal went in, you really start believing. Derby were a good side with some good players. Even getting a point out of the game was massive in the way that we did it. It was a big turning point for us.'

Had there been an extra five or ten minutes of time added on, Lee Camp wasn't alone in his thinking that Rotherham would have been walking away with all three points. Derby had reportedly spent £25m assembling a team to get them back into the top tier, but money couldn't buy the never-say-die attitude on display from Rotherham. And as the players geared up to head off on a planned night out in Leeds after the game, who could they possibly have stumbled across?

'The bar we were in that night, the Derby lads were in as well!' Newell remarks. 'That was a good little coincidence. We were speaking to them and they were raging at their manager because he took two of their main boys off and brought two other lads on who hadn't been going well.'

Rotherham were now hot on the heels of MK Dons, who played out a 1-1 draw with Hull City that same weekend. Fulham, who were relegated from the Premier League in the same season that Rotherham came up from League One, found themselves being dragged down by the current. Winless in their last five and having suffered back-to-back losses, the Cottagers were level with MK Dons on 37 points following a defeat to Bristol City, whilst Rotherham tallied 36. It was tight at the bottom of the Championship.

The last time the Millers produced a resurgence anything like the fightback they pulled off against Derby was in

October 2011, when Andy Scott's Rotherham side – on an eight-game winless streak at the time – came from 3-0 down away at Morecambe in League Two. Scott's men were on the brink of a sixth defeat in seven games until Lewis Grabban reduced the arrears. In the second half, Gareth Evans made it 3-2 before Alex Revell levelled with 64 minutes played.

It wasn't until December 2019 that Rotherham fans got the chance to witness something similar when they travelled to Solihull Moors in the second round of the FA Cup. Just when it looked as though the League One side were about to be dumped from the competition at the hands of their non-league opponents – who sat 46 league places below them – Paul Warne's Millers rose from the ashes.

Solihull were in the driving seat with over an hour played, holding a 3-0 lead over the Millers. Rotherham's Freddie Ladapo pulled a goal back with 15 minutes left and Michael Ihiekwe soon made it 3-2. Michael Smith was at the double late in the day, levelling in the 88th minute and going one better in added time to complete the comeback, seeing Rotherham advance to the next round in a stunning 4-3 victory.

It was the kind of game Warnock could look to for encouragement, also. In his first game in charge of Aberdeen in February 2024, the Dons had to come from 3-0 down against Motherwell to earn a 3-3 draw. If he'd done it once, he could do it again.

'Someone said to me, "I've been coming 20 years and I've never seen anything like that, Warnock!"' the boss said after the game against Derby.

'In the Championship, you shouldn't get a draw from 3-0 down, in fairness,' he explained. 'It should be game, set and match, but our never-say-die attitude is fabulous. Nothing worries me about opponents. I just think about ourselves, really. A lot of teams would have packed in and tried to keep it to three, but we haven't got that in us.'

In his programme notes for the next home game against Leeds United, Warnock reflected: 'Who knows just how valuable that point could turn out to be at the end of the season?' The game felt like a microcosm of the campaign. Rotherham were at a crossroads when Derby's third goal went in. They could either revert to type or they could show some resilience and fight back. Had they laid down and accepted their fate, would they have had the belief to go on and finish the job?

Saturday, 19 March 2016
Portman Road
EFL Championship
Ipswich Town 0
Rotherham United 1 (Best 44')

The tide was beginning to turn in Warnock's favour. After the Millers salvaged a point against Derby in a game that, at another stage of the season, would have almost certainly ended in defeat for Rotherham, they had the chance to break away from the bottom three.

MK Dons entertained third-placed Brighton & Hove Albion whilst the Millers paid a visit to Portman Road to take on Ipswich Town. There was plenty at stake for the eighth-placed Tractor Boys, who still had a chance of catching up to the promotion-chasing pack to sneak into the top six before the season reached its conclusion.

On the day, though, it was Rotherham who wanted it more. Even dressed in their vivid, all-yellow away strip, it appeared that teams still didn't see Warnock's side coming. The result against Mick McCarthy's Ipswich lifted the Millers out of the relegation zone for the first time since January.

Warnock made only minor tweaks to the team that had traded blows with the Rams. Grant Ward and Lloyd Doyley came into the side in place of Danny Collins and Paul

Green. Tottenham Hotspur prodigy Ward was concerned that Warnock might struggle to find a place for him within his system, with the Millers manager fielding the club's combined oldest starting line-up in the game against Derby since Ronnie Moore in 2003/04. But Ward, who would go on to win the club's young player of the season award, proved his worth to the manager.

'I thought with a new manager coming in, I needed to see if he liked me,' Ward comments. 'It was great for my development. Playing under different managers was good because you need to adapt to how they want to play, so that was something that helped me in my career. All the managers that came in ended up liking me.

'They [Warnock and Blackwell] just wanted to make us solid, then he let the forwards do their own thing. He'd seen the results and how many goals we'd conceded and he just said to the defence, "If the donkeys at the back can keep it down to two goals, we might have a chance." He said, "Just give it to the creative players and the rest of you keep it simple." He named the forwards and said "Just feed them" and it worked.'

It was a quiet opening to the game, as both sides settled into the contest. That was until Best – Rotherham's two-goal hero in the draw against Derby – popped up. Strike partner Derbyshire had a rush of energy, bursting forward down the right. He pinged the ball into the box, where Best had peeled away from his man. Best, who would go on to sign for the Tractor Boys after his short stint with Rotherham came to an end, got his body in front of Cole Skuse, making enough contact with the ball to divert it into the back of the net. Goalkeeper Bartosz Białkowski – the same stopper who Rotherham put six goals past near enough two years earlier to the day in March 2014 whilst Białkowski was with Notts County – was a bystander as Rotherham made it 1-0 with the interval fast approaching.

There was another familiar face on the pitch as Ben Pringle – who had joined Ipswich on loan from Fulham in February – was introduced in the 70th minute. The ball fell to the winger in space and he fluffed his lines from close range. A loud groan of frustration went up from the home fans, which summed up Ipswich's afternoon in a single syllable as Warnock bellowed instructions to his team from the touchline.

'I was on the wing, so I was near him,' Grand Ward explains. 'He just kept calling my name and I didn't really want to look over. I looked over and he's just smiling and he's making a hand gesture to make a smile. He said "Just smile." He's just telling me to enjoy the moment.'

That joy was infectious. It was apparent on Warnock's face at full time, just as it was painted across all of his players' features. Rotherham were well on their way now. Not only did the Millers nudge MK Dons back into the drop zone, but they also leapfrogged Fulham, too. They finished the day in 20th, now unbeaten in five league games under Warnock.

'We worked to our strengths and it suited the players we had at the time,' Broadfoot outlines. 'In Leon Best, Matt Derbyshire and Danny Ward, we had three top strikers at the time. We made our back four hard to beat, with Greg Halford right in front of us and then Frecks [Lee Frecklington] came back and he made a huge difference, coming back from injury, with his energy. It took a couple of results and then we believed. We'd nick a goal and there was a few 1-0 wins in there.

'With the teams we played – we played five of the top six at the time and beat them – it just showed that if we had a chance at the start of the season, we could have been up in the top half and pushing for the play-offs.'

Elsewhere, both Charlton Athletic and Bolton Wanderers – still in the relegation zone – suffered defeat. Charlton, who had recorded two wins and a draw so far in March, lost 3-0 to Sheffield Wednesday in their final game of the month. Things were looking even bleaker for Bolton, who were beaten 6-0 by Bristol City in Jimmy Phillips's first game in his role as interim boss. The Trotters were without a win in their last eight league games – two draws and six defeats – and things weren't about to improve any time soon for Wanderers.

The club had parted company with manager Neil Lennon earlier in the week. Things hadn't quite worked out for the Northern Irishman, who arrived at the club in October 2014. Wanderers managed only an 18th-placed finish under Lennon in 2014/15 and now they were on the verge of relegation. Lennon, who won three Scottish Premier League titles with Celtic and beat Barcelona in the Champions League, might have boasted an impressive CV, but he couldn't do it on an overcast day at Portman Road like Neil Warnock could.

'We are not out of the woods by a mile, but it is nice to see yourselves out of the bottom three and putting pressure on other teams,' Warnock told the club's official website after the game, keeping a level head while discussing the day's talking points.

'To go from the run that we were on of hardly winning any games to win four games like that against that opposition gave us belief that we could actually pull off this miracle and stay up,' Frecklington adds. 'They were huge results, especially against teams of that calibre.'

League table:

Position	*Club*	*Pl*	*GD*	*Pts*
20	Rotherham United	38	-18	39
21	Fulham	38	-7	38
22	MK Dons	38	-19	37
23	Charlton Athletic	38	-35	32
24	Bolton Wanderers	38	-32	26

Prior to Neil Warnock's arrival, there would have been little chance of a Millers boss making Football League headline sponsor Sky Bet's divisional manager of the month shortlist. But it didn't come as a shock when the 68-year-old's name was put forward for March's award as a nod to the monumental job he was doing in South Yorkshire. In fact, it would have been a huge oversight had the Rotherham manager been omitted from the line-up.

He was up against three equally impressive candidates in Burnley's Sean Dyche, Cardiff City's Russell Slade and former Rotherham manager Steve Evans, now of Leeds United. The Clarets had taken ten points from a possible 12 as Dyche's team edged closer to the title. Evans, on the other hand, made it three wins in four to herd Leeds away from the relegation battle. Last but not least, Slade – the man in the dugout when the Millers broke Orient hearts at Wembley – had taken seven points from four games with the Bluebirds. Not that any of that mattered. The trio didn't stand a chance against Warnock. It was the perfect way to round off a whirlwind month since his touchdown at the New York Stadium. Heading into April, Rotherham's fate was now back in their own hands.

It was another individual accolade to add to the mantelpiece for the veteran boss. For the seventh time in his career, Warnock was named as the Championship manager of the month. He won the award for the first time in December 2004 – the season of its inception – when his Sheffield United side registered four wins in five league outings during the festive period. He became the first person to win back-to-back accolades when he received the award in consecutive months between August and September 2005 with the Blades. Warnock – who has also picked up the award with Crystal Palace, QPR and Cardiff City – has scooped the manager of the month a record 11 times to date. But with great power comes great responsibility and Warnock had a duty not to let the so-called manager of the month curse come to pass. He would ensure no such jinx would befall his team.

Skipper Lee Frecklington, who bagged the winner against Middlesbrough towards the start of the month, was up for the player of the month award but the midfielder, who played every single minute of each of Rotherham's games in March, lost out to Burnley striker Sam Vokes.

Also nominated were Leeds United striker Mirco Antenucci and Sheffield Wednesday defender Tom Lees. However, they all fell short of Vokes, who notched four goals in as many games to fire Burnley to the top of the table before jetting off on international duty with Wales.

As Warnock posed for a photograph with his prize, he allowed himself and his team to take a moment to reflect on just how far they'd come in a short space of time, but then it was straight back to work for the Millers. Rotherham had a date in the diary with another of Warnock's ex-employers to kick off April and they were looking to carry their impressive form into the following month. The Millers had registered four wins and a draw in their last five league outings, and had dropped just two points from a possible 15. They had a higher purpose and nobody was going to stand in their way.

Chapter Eight

Great Escape

IF ROTHERHAM United could pull off what was now being referred to as 'the great escape', there was no denying that they weren't the first and wouldn't be the last club to claim to have achieved such a thing. On paper, teams had been in tighter spots than Rotherham, who found themselves six points adrift of safety three games into Warnock's reign. However, given the torrid time the club had endured prior to his arrival, it was almost inconceivable that anybody could save them from their fate. If they could just get over the line, it might well be the greatest of escapes.

The Millers only had to cast back their minds to the 2014/15 season when Leicester City pulled off their own great escape to retain their top-flight status for another year. However, it was only a prequel of what was to come for them. Bottom of the league at the end of March, having won just four games all season, Nigel Pearson's men pulled it out of the bag late in the day. The club went on a run that saw them win seven of their last nine Premier League matches and secure survival with a game to spare. Did anybody anticipate that the Foxes would lift the Premier League trophy just 12 months later? Probably not. But, as the saying goes, stranger things have happened.

Take, for example, goalkeeper Jimmy Glass's stoppage-time winner for Carlisle United against Plymouth Argyle on the last day of the 1998/99 campaign. The Cumbrians managed to beat the drop and keep their place in the Football League by the skin of their teeth when the Pilgrims paid a visit to Brunton Park, with nothing less than a win enough to keep Carlisle in the old Third Division. Time was ticking and the score was 1-1. Carlisle were awarded a corner kick with what was estimated to be around ten seconds left on the watch – ten seconds to save their season. Glass, who had joined the club on loan from Swindon Town, opted to come up for the set piece and it might just have been the best decision he's ever made. Of course, he rippled the net and the rest is history.

More often than not, in the build-up to said great escape, a poor run of results prompts a changing of the guard, as it did for Rotherham when they replaced Neil Redfearn with Neil Warnock. Likewise, back in October 2013, Sunderland swapped Paolo Di Canio for Gus Poyet. The Black Cats were lodged in the relegation zone by April with an unenviable run-in on the horizon, leaving Poyet to conclude that it would take a 'miracle' for them to dodge the drop. They did it, though, the survival-clinching game coming against Chelsea as Poyet's men ended José Mourinho's 77-game unbeaten streak at Stamford Bridge.

It goes without saying that there is a fine line between hope and false hope. Even Warnock had to be realistic in his objectives, but – as he explained – he wouldn't have accepted the position if he thought it was beyond his capabilities to keep the club in the Championship. A rousing speech, like the one he issued to his Rotherham players, usually does the trick. In 2004/05, when West Bromwich Albion were bottom of the pile in the Premier League at Christmas, boss Bryan Robson was up front about the dire situation they were in, but the former England captain wasn't quite ready to give up the ghost just yet. He reasoned that the Baggies would 'just have to prove that the impossible can be made possible'. It was the kind of fighting talk that spoke West Brom's chances into existence.

Although Warnock's arrival in South Yorkshire gave the club a boost, a quick sweep over Rotherham's final fixtures was enough to fill them with a fresh sense of dread, just when they felt like the odds couldn't be stacked any higher against them. The same could have been said for Roberto Martínez's Wigan Athletic side in March 2012. The Premier League Latics still had four of the top six to play and not many people were expecting them to come away with seven wins in their last nine games, including victories away at Anfield and the Emirates, along with a shock 1-0 win over Manchester United on home soil. Such was also the case for the Millers, who took points from the likes of promotion-chasing Middlesbrough, Derby County, Sheffield Wednesday and Ipswich Town along the way.

For some teams, it's simply too little, too late but, fortunately, Warnock's team hit their stride in the nick of time. The Millers' 11-game unbeaten streak – which included six wins and five draws – was ultimately what kept their heads above water. Rewind to 1957/58 when Lincoln City won their last six games in the old Second Division – having lost nine on the spin prior to that – as they fought to keep their place in the league. And in 2014/15, Leicester harvested seven wins and a draw from their last nine Premier League games to reverse their fortunes.

Sometimes, all it takes is one result to turn things around. In May 2008, Roy Hodgson's Fulham found themselves 2-0 down at Manchester City with 20 minutes of the game remaining, only to complete an astonishing comeback which saw the Cottagers win the game 3-2 and go on to escape the drop. For Rotherham, the 3-3 draw at home to Derby County immediately springs to mind. Of course, there were memorable victories over Yorkshire rivals Sheffield

Wednesday, Middlesbrough and Leeds United, along with a huge win against relegation rivals MK Dons, but there was something to be said for the scenes at the New York Stadium when Leon Best found the net in added time as everything came together for the club.

* * *

It was a crucial interval for Rotherham, whose season still hung in the balance. All it would take was one result to go against them and tip the scales in their relegation rivals' favour or vice versa. They were not home and dry just yet. Warnock's side could just as easily lose their footing and take a tumble back into the relegation zone.

'A few friends told me I was mad and to go and get a part in *One Flew Over the Cuckoo's Nest*. I'm the man who once turned down Chelsea to stay at Notts County. I am a nutter, aren't I?' said Warnock in an article in the *Sheffield Star* after the game against Wolverhampton, explaining that he had questioned his own sanity since taking the Rotherham job. It was all about to pay off for Warnock and what came next went down as one of his best – if not his best – achievements in football as the home stretch set up a thrilling season finale.

Saturday, 2 April 2016
New York Stadium
EFL Championship
Rotherham United 2 (Frecklington 27', Halford 90')
Leeds United 1 (Murphy 79')
When Steve Evans returned to the New York Stadium for the first time since leaving his post as the Rotherham manager in September 2015, he was hoping to prevent the Millers from doing the double over Leeds United. Nevertheless, the Scot received a warm welcome at his old stomping ground as the

Leeds boss reciprocated by wishing Warnock's team well for the remainder of the campaign.

Warnock, like predecessor Neil Redfearn, had a history with the Whites. In February 2012, Warnock inked a deal with Leeds which would see him become the club's new manager until the end of the 2012/13 season, picking up where caretaker boss Redfearn left off. Leeds finished up in 14th place in the Championship at the end of the 2011/12 season and Warnock's time in West Yorkshire came to an end just over a year later, with the club unhappy with his progress after a run of defeats.

'I don't say this with any disrespect to the other teams I have managed, but Leeds are the biggest club I have taken charge of,' Warnock said in his programme notes for the game against the Whites.

Despite the mutual air of positivity, both bosses were feeling the pressure. Leeds' form under Evans had been largely inconsistent, while Warnock was fully aware of what was at stake for Rotherham.

Lee Frecklington might have missed his chance to score against his boyhood club last time out at Elland Road, but he was fired up once again in the reverse fixture. With 27 minutes played, the midfielder connected with Joe Mattock's ball in from the left. The skipper managed to get something on it and watched the ball beat the outstretched frame of Marco Silvestri to make it 1-0 to the hosts.

'Unfortunately, I never got to play for Leeds, but playing against them and scoring against them is as close as it gets to what I wanted to do as a kid,' Frecklington says. 'I remember the cross came in from Joe Mattock and I just slid in at the back stick.

'It was the next best feeling. The elation you feel to score against your boyhood team is something that I still remember to this day.'

It was fair to say that Leeds had the better of the second half. Rotherham were reduced to ten men after Matt Derbyshire received his first-ever red card in English football. The striker was dismissed for what referee Kevin Friend saw as a deliberate elbow, which left defender Gaetano Berardi with a bloodied face. The red card would later be overturned following a successful appeal. However, the Millers were outnumbered and it showed, especially when Luke Murphy got the visitors back on terms with around ten minutes left. The deflected strike caught goalkeeper Lee Camp off guard and it was 1-1 at the New York.

However, it only drove Rotherham on. Frecklington looked certain to grab his and the Millers' second of the afternoon when he latched on to Danny Ward's cross, only to be tripped by Silvestri before he could pull the trigger. Friend pointed to the spot and dismissed the Leeds goalkeeper. With Leeds out of substitutions, defender Giuseppe Bellusci pulled on Silvestri's neon green goalkeeping jersey and prepared to go up against Greg Halford as a makeshift keeper. Halford dispatched the spot kick, sending Bellusci the wrong way and rolling the ball into the bottom left-hand corner.

'I scored the first one and then I got brought down for the penalty late on, so I was desperate to get the ball,' Frecklington explains. 'Greg was one of Neil's favourites and all I could hear from the touchline was "Let Greg take it!" You can't really go against Neil Warnock, can you? What he said, we all did at that time. I handed the ball over to Greg and, thankfully, he tucked it away and we won the game.'

Evans later explained after the game that he didn't believe anyone inside the ground, including both sets of fans, could see anything other than Leeds going on to win the game after the break, but it didn't matter – Warnock's side had once again found a way to win.

'Frecks had scored the first one, then they levelled up with a decent goal,' Halford adds. 'Frecks wins a penalty in the last five minutes and he wanted to take it, but I was designated penalty taker and I wasn't giving it up. Frecks was a Leeds supporter and he'd already scored one. It was a sweet moment, but the three points was the only thing we were after from that game.'

Leeds would be the only team Rotherham completed a league double over that season after beating the Whites 1-0 away from home in Redfearn's first game in charge. Evans was eventually sacked in late May after seven months at the helm, with chairman Massimo Cellino saying that he wanted to go in a different direction ahead of the new campaign.

Meanwhile, Warnock allowed Tom Thorpe to go out on loan to Bradford City, with the defender having made seven appearances since joining in the summer, scoring two goals in the process. The boss had established his core group of players and he was sticking with it. Although it wasn't necessarily what he was used to – battling against the drop at the wrong end of the table – Warnock's blueprint for promotion could still be applied to Rotherham's bid for survival. All he needed were some strong characters and a bit of application from his players, and Warnock was on his way.

'I don't know if I can carry on doing much more like this – my heart is taking a beating,' he told the club's official website after the game. 'Three-nil down against Derby and this, today. I need a good medical at the end of the season.'

He also admitted that his team would have to 'scrap for every point' but insisted they were more than willing to do so. Rotherham, who had trailed MK Dons by six points after losing to Reading at the end of February, now had a five-point advantage on their relegation rivals. It wasn't job done just yet, but it was progress for the Millers, who had come a long way under Warnock.

Tuesday, 5 April 2016
Ashton Gate
EFL Championship
Bristol City 1 (Odemwingie 54')
Rotherham United 1 (Derbyshire 12')

It was to be expected that the Rotherham boss would have a history with teams up and down the country, including those clubs he'd personally managed and those he'd simply crossed paths with his during his career in the dugout. One such team was Bristol City, who it just so happened the Millers would come up against while riding the wave of a six-game unbeaten streak.

It was a feud that dated back to 2008 when Warnock's Crystal Palace spent the 2007/08 season battling it out for promotion with Gary Johnson's Robins. In the end, Palace were beaten by Bristol City in the play-off semi-final before Johnson's men lost out to Hull City in the final. The pair clashed again in August 2009 over Freddie Sears's famous 'phantom goal' for Palace against Bristol City. The striker found the back of the net for Palace, only for the ball to hit the stanchion and bounce straight back out and, with no goal-line technology in operation at the time, the goal wasn't given. It led Warnock to criticise Johnson's sportsmanship after Bristol City went on to win the game 1-0.

Warnock – who reignited his rivalry with the club when he later took charge at Cardiff City in the Severnside derby – drew a few laughs when he famously declared: 'When I pass away, I don't want clapping or a minute's silence, I want a minute's booing at Bristol City.'

Ironically, it was the former City manager's son, Lee Johnson – who was on the bench that day in August 2009 – in the hotseat when Warnock visited Ashton Gate with the Millers in April 2016. In his post-match press conference, the Rotherham manager came equipped with cuttings of Johnson junior's pre-match comments, which Warnock had used to motivate his Rotherham players ahead of their midweek jaunt. In the run-up to the game, Johnson told the *Bristol Post* that he had urged his players to win the game through 'aggression, good football or intimidation'. Warnock insisted he was proud of the way in which the Millers stood up to the opposition and their attempts at 'inciting the crowd'.

With the news that Derbyshire's red card had been rescinded, the striker kept his place in the starting line-up and, just 12 minutes in, fired Rotherham into the lead. A long ball lofted upfield by Wood – described as a 'Beckenbauer pass' by Warnock – found Derbyshire in behind the defence. His first touch brought the ball under control and, with two red shirts bearing down on him and Bristol City keeper Richard O'Donnell coming out to meet him, Derbyshire chipped the Sheffield-born stopper – who would later become a Rotherham player in January 2017 – to make it 1-0.

At the other end of the pitch, the Millers were indebted to Camp for keeping them in the contest. The keeper made a string of stops. All of them were strong contenders for the save of the season, but his single-handed effort to keep out Aden Flint's header from a corner was as good as any of the game-saving moments he'd produced over the course of the season.

But he couldn't keep out Peter Odemwingie in the 54th minute. Scott Golbourne's delivery into the box was cleared only as far as Odemwingie, who reacted fastest to smash home the leveller. With ten minutes left to play, Odemwingie was all but ready to celebrate his second goal of the evening before Camp's reflexes kicked in once again.

The Millers, who had been humbling teams since Warnock arrived, were now six points clear of the drop zone after Wolverhampton Wanderers did the Millers a favour by beating MK Dons on the same night Rotherham played out their 1-1 draw with Bristol City. The heat was well and truly on.

Saturday, 9 April 2016
Stadium MK
EFL Championship

MK Dons 0

Rotherham United 4 (Derbyshire 1', Best 17', Broadfoot 54', Smallwood 79')

Not that the Millers needed any extra motivation heading into a clash with their fiercest relegation rivals but if they did, it was provided by MK Dons defender George Baldock. Just as Rotherham had been keeping tabs on results elsewhere, so were Karl Robinson's men. After losing to Wolves in midweek – while Rotherham picked up a point at Bristol City – Baldock admitted 'there were a few moans and groans' when the MK Dons players heard that the Millers' unbeaten run had lived to see another day. As they prepared for the visit of Warnock's team in four days' time, the full-back added that, despite Rotherham's seemingly unstoppable form, the Millers were 'not Real Madrid' and they would 'slip up eventually'. The Dons, he said, would need to be ready and waiting when they did.

Baldock's comments weren't dissimilar to Millwall striker Lee Gregory's remarks at the back end of the 2014/15 campaign when the striker said he hoped that Steve Evans's side would 'bottle it' to allow Millwall to keep their place in the Championship. In the end, Rotherham's victory over Reading sent the Lions down to League One and Evans answered back after the game, explaining that he had '12 bottles of pink champagne' which he would use to toast the Millers' safety.

Now, it was Warnock's men against the world. While everyone was expecting Rotherham to stumble at some stage and derail their efforts, it wasn't about to happen any time soon. It was no fluke that they had been unbeaten in their last seven outings – five of which were wins – but if opposition comments called for Rotherham to show just why they deserved to be a Championship team the following season, they were about to elicit a response.

If there was a date in the diary to be circled not once but twice and underlined in red marker pen, it was Rotherham's trip to Buckinghamshire. It had already been established that the Millers simply needed to beat as many teams as realistically possible before the season was out to give themselves a fighting chance, but if ever there was a must-win game, it was this one. Victory by any means would have ensured Warnock's side took a huge stride towards safety, but a 4-0 drubbing – the club's joint most comprehensive victory of the season – sent out a message loud and clear that Rotherham were serious about staying in the Championship.

The two clubs had previous, too. On the final day of the 2005/06 season, a goalless draw with Danny Wilson's MK Dons – who needed a win to stay up – secured Rotherham's League One status under then-manager Alan Knill at the cost of the Buckinghamshire team's place in the division. However, the Millers already knew they would be starting the following term on minus ten points – no matter which league they were in – which would be imposed when they entered administration.

Fast forward ten years. With Rotherham's season potentially riding on the game against MK Dons – who had ex-Millers man Alex Revell starting up front – there were feelings of apprehension bubbling before kick-off, but Millers striker Derbyshire eased any tension just 54 seconds in when he rippled the net. Grant Ward led the attack for Rotherham, using his pace to burst down the right and send a low cross in for Derbyshire. His initial effort was saved by keeper Cody Cropper before the forward blasted the rebound into the roof of the net. He was never going to miss from there.

Derbyshire says: 'That was one of the games where I thought, "Warnock's set his mark and we're really playing well here." I remember the way we were passing the ball around on such a massive field. When we'd scored, we'd keep the ball a bit more and, instead of defending the lead, we were going for more.'

The goal was Derbyshire's eighth of the campaign and that tally would see him crowned the club's leading marksman for the second season in a row, falling just two short of his ten goals in all competitions from 2014/15. It wasn't to be sniffed at for a striker playing in a struggling side and, although his contributions might have gone under the radar at times, they couldn't be downplayed. Not to mention Derbyshire had big shoes to fill, following on from Kieran Agard's 26-goal haul in 2013/14 before the forward signed for Bristol City in the summer of 2014.

The last time Rotherham were in the Championship, it was Martin Butler – who bagged 15 goals in the old First Division during the 2003/04 season – leading the line. Before Butler, there was Mark Robins – the former Millers manager whose goals fired Rotherham into the second tier and kept them there – and Alan Lee, who scored one of the most famous goals in Rotherham's history. Lee found the back of the net with a last-gasp winner against Brentford on the penultimate day of the 2000/01 season to clinch promotion to the second tier.

'The chances didn't come thick and fast as they have at other clubs,' Derbyshire continues. 'When you score, you wanted to defend that scoreline. We made the most of every game when we scored first to try and get the three points. Scoring is my job, but trying to get three points first and foremost was the main task.

'After that game, I remember going "Phwoar, that's a massive weight off my shoulders." Warnock said, "Two or three days off now, lads, and we'll be back in to work as usual." Even throughout the season when we'd win, when we were supposed to be in on a Sunday, he'd go, "Don't bother coming in. Great result – you can have Sunday and Monday off and be back in on Tuesday."'

In the 17th minute, Rotherham were awarded a penalty after Richard Wood was taken out by Cropper as he raced off his line. Warnock had options when it came to penalties. Halford and Frecklington had been the go-to takers at different points during the season, but it was Leon Best who stepped up to make it four goals in five games for the striker as he expertly tucked the spot kick into the right-hand corner to double the Millers' advantage. It was a dream start.

'That was the most away goals we'd scored for ages,' Wood explains. 'Broady scored a great header, with the fans behind the goal. I won the penalty in the first half. I was brought down, which is unlike me because I can't dive anyway, but he definitely took me out!'

Warnock's side settled for 2-0 at half-time and there was more to come in the second period. So often the saviour at one end of the pitch, Kirk Broadfoot opened his account for the club at the other, rising highest to glance Joe Newell's cross into the far corner and make it 3-0. It had close to 3,000 away fans tucked into the corner of Stadium MK racing out of their seats to celebrate with the defender. The Millers could taste victory and, above all, they were within touching distance of pulling off the greatest escape.

However, Richie Smallwood's 79th-minute strike was, without a doubt, the pick of the bunch. The midfielder finished off a move that ended with him unexpectedly letting fly from outside the box, around 20 yards out from the target. Nobody was expecting Smallwood, of all the players on the pitch, to take aim from such a distance, but confidence wasn't something Warnock's players were in short supply of anymore. The home supporters headed for the exits, but the Rotherham contingent was going nowhere – the travelling fans were set on showing their players some appreciation at the full-time whistle.

'I didn't talk with Smallwood about his goal. I talked about how he could miss a point-blank header!' Warnock laughed after the game. 'I've forgot about his goal, so he may not be too happy when I see him.'

Now nine points clear of MK Dons, Rotherham left Buckinghamshire with six wins from their last eight league outings on the back of their latest conquest. Just as Warnock's men were picking up the pace, MK Dons took a nosedive. Defeat against Rotherham was the Dons' fourth loss on the spin. Robinson's men were without a win in their last six and they wouldn't taste victory again for the remainder of the season. The long-serving MK Dons boss – who said he felt 'sick' in the wake of the result against Rotherham – was sacked the following season, with his team sitting 19th in League One by October.

Little did Rotherham know it was a feeling they should savour, too. The Millers would have to wait until September 2017 – a barren 27-game streak – for their next victory on the road, beating Portsmouth 1-0 at Fratton Park after eventually suffering relegation back to League One. The next time they'd win away from home in the Championship would be in March 2019 when Paul Warne's Millers ran out 2-1 winners over QPR at Loftus Road.

Elsewhere, Bolton Wanderers became the first side to be relegated from the Championship. Derby County delivered the fatal blow as the game at Pride Park ended in a 4-1 defeat for the Trotters, who hadn't been in the third tier since 1992/93. It was one less team to worry about for Rotherham as they closed in on Championship survival.

And although the Millers were no Spanish giants, in a stroke of irony, Real Madrid – the team Baldock had mentioned in the same breath as Rotherham – also ran out 4-0 winners over Eibar at the Santiago Bernabéu on the same day that the Millers vanquished MK Dons. James Rodríguez's stylish free kick was the standout strike for Real Madrid, but it wasn't a patch on Smallwood's piledriver.

League table:

Position	*Club*	*Pl*	*GD*	*Pts*
20	Nottingham Forest	40	-6	46
21	Rotherham United	41	-13	46
22	MK Dons	41	-25	37
23	Charlton Athletic	41	-35	36
24	Bolton Wanderers	41	-38	26

Saturday, 16 April 2016
New York Stadium
EFL Championship
Rotherham United 0
Nottingham Forest 0

It was almost 20 years to the day that the Millers graced the home of English football for the very first time. Division Two side Rotherham ran out 2-1 winners over Shrewsbury Town in the 1996 Auto Windscreens Shield Trophy at the old Wembley Stadium. Under the joint management of Archie Gemmill and John McGovern, the club got its hands on a first piece of silverware. The pair, who had won the European Cup with Nottingham Forest – with McGovern twice captaining the Tricky Trees to victory in the competition – gave Rotherham supporters a day to remember and the Forest connections didn't end there. Nigel Jemson – who netted the winning goal for Forest in the 1990 League Cup Final – was at the double for the Millers at the national stadium. And some of those Wembley winners were in attendance at the

New York Stadium when the Millers welcomed Nottingham Forest to South Yorkshire to mark the anniversary of their first Wembley trip.

Similarly, despite winning plenty of medals and trophies along the way during his career, if Warnock could keep Rotherham in the Championship, it would trump everything that had gone before.

During his own playing days, Warnock was a pacey winger, albeit a bit of a journeyman. Nevertheless, when he hung up his boots for good aged 30 to take his first steps into football management, he'd amassed over 300 league appearances while playing for the likes of Chesterfield – where he started his career – Rotherham, Hartlepool United, Scunthorpe United, Aldershot, Barnsley, York City and Crewe Alexandra. One of his best spells, though, came at Rotherham. The club's first summer signing in 1969 from Chesterfield, Warnock – who spent his teenage years working in accounts and at a local bowling alley before getting his break with the Spireites – played his part in a record-equalling 18-game unbeaten run that the Millers went on between October 1969 and February 1970 in the old Third Division. There wasn't quite enough time for him to match that sequence as a manager in 2016, but he wouldn't be far off if he could keep the streak alive.

The boss named an unchanged team for a third successive game on the back of a draw with Bristol City and a win over MK Dons. Both teams were satisfied with a point when the Millers and the Reds played out a goalless draw at the New York. They were tied on 47 points, separated only by goal difference with four games remaining.

Stopper Camp was at his best against another of his former clubs as a last-ditch save to deny Ryan Mendes stretched Rotherham's run to nine games without defeat. It earned the keeper the man of the match award, along with a rendition of 'There's only one Lee Camp'. He wasn't the only one who put in a shift between the sticks that afternoon, either. MK prolonged their stay in the division with a 1-1 draw against Preston North End. They owed a debt of gratitude to former Rotherham man Alex Revell, who donned the goalkeeping gloves to save a penalty in the 81st minute. When Cody Cropper was sent off for the Dons, Revell acted as a stand-in stopper and ended up saving Joe Garner's spot kick to preserve a point.

At the end of the Millers' game, Warnock gave Richard Wood – who hadn't found the back of the net since April 2015 during a loan spell with Crawley Town – a glimpse of the match ball to show the defender what he should have been going home with. Wood missed a string of headers – five, for those who were keeping count – one of which rattled the bar from close range. He should have had a hat-trick, but a point was better than none. After all, it bettered the club's points tally from 2014/15 when Rotherham avoided the drop under Evans on 46 points despite a late points deduction which put the season on tenterhooks.

To put it into context, in 11 games with Warnock in charge, Rotherham had accumulated 20 points, compared to the 25 points they picked up in the 30 games prior to his appointment. It was still mathematically possible for the Millers to finish inside the top ten and, with Warnock at the helm, it wasn't beyond the realms of possibility if they carried on the way they were going.

In light of recent performances, there were a couple of disgruntled fans in the stands who were most likely hoping to see a rerun of the show the Millers put on against MK Dons. In his programme notes for the following game against Huddersfield Town, Warnock recounted how he responded to the supporter behind the dugout whose cry of 'rubbish' reached him on the touchline. 'Where have you been the last few games?' Warnock had asked him.

Tuesday, 19 April 2016
New York Stadium
EFL Championship
Rotherham United 1 (Halford 10')
Huddersfield Town 1 (Wells 22')

Warnock was enjoying his time back in the saddle so much that it wasn't long before he confirmed he would be in a dugout somewhere the following season. But the question was where? If Rotherham had their wish, it would, of course, be the New York Stadium, but Warnock's stock was high. Despite facing an uncertain future, the boss was helping to get matters in order for 2016/17 – whether that be laying the foundations for a new manager or getting himself a head start should he choose to stay on in South Yorkshire. He advised chairman Tony Stewart on improvements to the club's infrastructure and the training ground – which needed some work – while he mulled over his impending decision. Warnock later told the *Yorkshire Post* that, although the club wouldn't win any prizes for their facilities, his job was to 'make them feel like Wembley' for the players. And if there was one thing he was good at, it was being resourceful.

His time at Rotherham had whetted the appetite. It could be likened to his stint at Third Division side Torquay United in 1992/93. After being sacked by Notts County – the club he took all the way to the top flight via consecutive promotions from the Third to the First Division – Warnock initially joined Torquay as a consultant. He received a call a few weeks after the dust had settled on his departure from Meadow Lane and was brought in to offer his assistance to first-team manager Paul Compton. However, in the wake of Compton's dismissal, Warnock offered to step in, despite being warned against it, as he recalled in his autobiography, *Made in Sheffield*. Concerns were expressed about the damage it might do to his reputation if he failed to keep Torquay – who were in serious danger of dropping out of the professional pyramid – in the league. Who would offer him employment in the world of football management if Torquay were relegated? But he was nothing if not a risk-taker. The Gulls stayed up with victory over Carlisle in their penultimate game of the season and Warnock's love for the game had been restored.

Rotherham's unbeaten streak reached double figures, with Huddersfield the next side in line to test their resolve. The Terriers were another of Warnock's ex-employers. Back in the summer of 1995, just days after guiding Huddersfield to Wembley glory in the Second Division play-off final – where they beat Bristol Rovers – he quit the Terriers and linked up with recently relegated Plymouth Argyle. It was a time when everything he touched turned to gold, Warnock returning to the home of football the following season with Plymouth, who won promotion via the Third Division play-off final against Darlington.

Little did the Terriers – who shocked the football world when they won promotion to the Premier League the following season – know that a few years down the line, they'd be needing a sprinkle of that Warnock magic to get them out of a similar predicament in a run-in which would rival Rotherham's own.

Halford had a helping hand in the opening goal for Rotherham after ten minutes. Huddersfield couldn't deal with Mattock's corner and when the ball was headed back across goal, Halford's strike took a deflection off Dean Whitehead before hitting Terriers keeper Jed Steer on its way into the net.

'He put me in a position where I could create and still end up scoring at the same time, so it was a good fit,' Halford recalls. 'He had that team chemistry. We made very few changes to our starting XI for those 15 games he was in charge. It was like playing for a whole new club.

'Nobody gave us a hope in hell to win these games and we were just batting teams away, I wouldn't say easily, but a few months before, we had no chance against these teams. I swear, I don't know how Warnock does it, but he gets everyone fighting for each other. That's why he's had so much success over his career. He is an absolute genius.'

Later in the first half, Grant Ward had his pocket picked in his own half and when the ball was threaded through to Nahki Wells, the striker made it 1-1. It wasn't the Millers at their best and Warnock knew that, acknowledging there were some 'below par' performances from his players, but a little bit of fatigue was to be expected. His players were running on empty with the end of the season in sight and Warnock could only take his hat off to them. All would quickly be forgiven and forgotten.

Despite being held to a draw, they were nearly there. Had Rotherham bettered MK Dons' result and matched Charlton's, survival would have been confirmed that same night. Charlton fell to the sword in a 0-0 stalemate against already relegated Bolton Wanderers. There was no way back for the Addicks, who needed no less than a win against the Trotters to keep their dwindling hopes of survival alive. Meanwhile, MK Dons played out a goalless draw with Sheffield Wednesday and the Millers were made to wait. However, with Rotherham in the form of their lives, it was only a matter of time.

The unbeaten streak matched that of the class of 1981/82, managed by the late Emlyn Hughes. The former player-manager also oversaw a run of ten games without defeat in the second tier, including nine straight victories, with a side that included the likes of John Breckin, Tony Towner and Ronnie Moore. But Warnock was determined to go one better when his team travelled to the West Midlands just four days later.

Saturday, 23 April 2016
Molineux
EFL Championship
Wolverhampton Wanderers 0
Rotherham United 0

It had been 50 years since Jack Mansell's Millers went 11 games unbeaten at the same level in 1965/66 – 50 years since a Rotherham team had managed 11 games without defeat in the second tier of English football. The class of 2015/16 equalled a club record. And the added bonus, you ask? They achieved the small matter of securing their place in the division for another season. There were certain similarities between the current crop and Mansell's team, too. As fate would have it, Rotherham mounted a late surge between February and April 1966 in the Second Division – the same period that Warnock oversaw in 2016.

The Millers went on to finish seventh in the league that season, with the sequence coming to an end against eventual champions Manchester City. During that run, there were wins against Derby County, Bury, Norwich City (twice) and Bolton Wanderers, plus draws with Coventry City, Cardiff City, Southampton, Preston North End, Portsmouth and Ipswich Town. During the Warnock era, the Millers beat Brentford, Sheffield Wednesday, Middlesbrough, Ipswich Town, Leeds United and MK Dons, and drew with Derby County, Bristol City, Nottingham Forest, Huddersfield Town and Wolverhampton Wanderers.

The game itself against Wolves was uneventful. It was a far cry from previous visits to Molineux. The two sides had played out a ten-goal thriller in the West Midlands during the 2013/14 campaign as both teams battled it out for promotion from League One. Wanderers ran out 6-4 winners that day as they edged closer to automatic promotion, but neither set of fans could complain that they weren't entertained.

Fast forward two years and a tame stalemate was something the Millers would have snapped off your hand for prior to kick-off. There would be no full-scale pitch invasion, no last-minute theatrics and no sombreros kicking about. The result against Wolves felt more like a formality than anything else after the mammoth shift Warnock's men put in against MK Dons. An anti-climax? Maybe. There were chants of 'boring' ringing around the stadium from the home fans, but the Rotherham supporters didn't care. It didn't need to be a classic in their eyes.

Dressed in a mash-up of their second and third kits – comprising navy blue shirts and socks with yellow shorts – due to a colour clash with Wolves' strip, the Millers got under way at Molineux backed by 668 travelling fans who made the trip down to the West Midlands. The hosts appeared to have misplaced their shooting boots, having failed to ripple the net at Molineux since early March and that suited the Millers, who only needed a point to confirm their survival, just fine. As it transpired, Rotherham's result was rendered irrelevant after MK Dons lost 4-1 to Brentford, meaning they would be joining Charlton Athletic and Bolton Wanderers in League One for the 2016/17 season, while Rotherham would remain a Championship team.

The sight of experienced defensive duo Wood and Broadfoot patched up and held together by medical dressings and surgical tape to keep them in one piece for the duration of the next 90 minutes and get the Millers over the finish line just about summed them up. Rotherham made it five clean sheets in six games. Not bad for a team who, not so long ago, couldn't stop conceding goals no matter how hard they tried. They had tightened up at the back and found a way to break teams down. It was simple but effective.

Wood recalls: 'I remember me and Broady both banged our heads – not together – but we'd got knocks and had to have bandages on our heads during the games. For the last few games, we both wore red headbands. It was coloured tape – normally it's white or black – but we had red tape, which was to do with the red sock tape that we wore to match the kit and the Rotherham colours. For the last few games of the season, all of the fans started wearing red headbands! It was a thing that we got going and fans were loving it because me and Broady were wearing red headbands every game.

'That summed up our way of playing with grit and determination. Me and Broady were hard as nails at the back and weren't bothered by a cut on our heads. We just got on with it. Fans took to it and started coming to games with headbands on, like the Terry Butcher strapping. That sort of camaraderie between us and the fans was good.'

Now up to 19th in the table, Warnock's men could finally breathe a sigh of relief. To put the run into context, only five other teams in the division had managed to go ten consecutive games without defeat over the course of the campaign and, not surprisingly, it was the teams who finished in the top five: Burnley, Middlesbrough, Brighton & Hove Albion, Hull City and Derby County. What's more, only three of these had put together a run of 11 games or more without a loss. Those teams were Burnley, who ended the season 23 games unbeaten, Brighton, whose streak stretched to 21 games, and Hull, who matched Rotherham's 11-game sequence.

'From where we were, I'd say it was more relief,' Danny Ward reflects. 'When you're in that position, anything can happen in the Championship. That's the mental side of football, isn't it? It shows how quickly things can turn around. We might have been in a completely different position if the gaffer had come in earlier that season. It's just as good when you're struggling at the bottom and manage to stay in the league.'

There would be a chance to give Warnock and his men a heroes' welcome home to the New York Stadium – and the reception they deserved – when Blackburn Rovers visited in a week's time in the penultimate game of the campaign. There was still plenty to play for in the top half of the table but with the bottom three done and dusted, the Millers could sit back and relax to an extent.

The boss – who was serenaded with a chorus of 'Neil Warnock is a Red' at Molineux – told the press afterwards that he had a driver taking him back to Cornwall that evening so that the Rotherham manager could crack open a bottle of bubbly on the journey home. And in equalling a club record, he was well aware that what he and his players had achieved would go down in history.

'They've talked about a reunion in 20 years, but I mentioned to Derbs [Matt Derbyshire] that I might not be here then!' he laughed in response.

League table:

Position	*Club*	*Pl*	*GD*	*Pts*
19	Rotherham United	44	-13	49
20	Bristol City	44	-20	49
21	Fulham	44	-11	48
22	MK Dons	44	-28	39
23	Charlton Athletic	44	-38	37
24	Bolton Wanderers	44	-40	27

After achieving what, 73 days earlier, had seemed like the impossible – delivering the promise of a third successive season in the Championship – the final home game of the campaign was where the unbeaten streak met its maker. While there have been a number of impressive runs since – perhaps most notably, the 21-game unbeaten sequence that the League One club put together in all competitions in 2021/22 when Rotherham secured promotion and won the EFL Trophy at Wembley – the emotional roller-coaster of 2015/16 and the great escape was unparalleled. It was a season that had everything: the highs, the lows and everything in between.

It was mission accomplished and it had taken just about every ounce of blood, sweat and tears to get it over the line, but there was still 180 minutes left of football to play and Warnock and his players were going to embrace every second of it. After all, it could be the last time they'd be together as a team.

Chapter Nine

Foot Off the Gas

HAD NEIL Warnock overseen Rotherham United from the start of the 2015/16 season, the Millers could well have been on the brink of the play-offs – as many of his players had already suggested when they were at the peak of their powers – rather than teetering just above the relegation zone. By the end of his short reign, his side were averaging 1.5 points per game, taking 24 points from Warnock's 16 games in charge. That compared to around 0.83 prior to the experienced manager exiting retirement to come to Rotherham's rescue. Of course, over the course of a full campaign, a team's form ebbs and flows, but in the three months Warnock had been at the helm, the Millers boss had the players pushing their potential. Looking forward, anything appeared possible if the club could keep hold of Warnock. With a few tweaks to the existing squad in the summer, why couldn't Rotherham go for broke the following season? The 2016/17 campaign couldn't come soon enough if that was the case. He had the club daring to dream once again.

He still had two games left to make the most of the here and now before he had a decision to make about his future. The Millers entertained Blackburn Rovers at the New York Stadium before travelling to East Yorkshire to end the season away at Hull City. Warnock didn't want to tempt fate by saying that his team were aiming to finish the campaign by continuing their unbeaten run, but it wasn't too much to ask his players for one last push to go out on a high – if not for him, then for themselves.

Saturday, 30 April 2016
New York Stadium
EFL Championship
Rotherham United 0
Blackburn Rovers 1 (Duffy 6')

Rotherham were already mathematically safe following the previous weekend's goalless draw against Wolverhampton Wanderers, meaning they could enjoy their final home game without the thought of relegation weighing on their minds. It was a luxury nobody was expecting prior to Warnock's arrival. And if there was one thing Rotherham had to be thankful for, it was the avoidance of any late surprises. Their fate had been signed, sealed and delivered. On the final day of the 2013/14 campaign, as Rotherham were gearing up for the play-offs, Birmingham City caught the headlines when a 93rd-minute equaliser from Paul Caddis in a 2-2 draw with Bolton Wanderers saw the Blues stay up, while the Millers' local rivals, Doncaster Rovers, were relegated back to League One by virtue of the result. It was no doubt entertaining for the neutral but, thankfully, Rotherham had steered clear of any such spectacle.

With the Millers occupying 19th place and Blackburn Rovers guaranteed to finish comfortably in mid-table – sitting in 15th as it stood – it might have looked like a game in which neither team had much to play for, but it meant so much more than that to the Millers.

When the club had hosted MK Dons on the opening day of the campaign, slumping to a 4-1 defeat, it was apparent that it was going to be a long season. Nobody – not Steve Evans, Neil Redfearn, Neil Warnock, Tony Stewart, the fans or the players – knew quite what to expect between August

2015 and May 2016, but they knew it would be a slog. Three managers, 25 defeats in all competitions and one unforgettable unbeaten run later, they'd reached the finish line. There was no Wembley trip, no medals, no trophy to lift at the end of it, but there was a set of supporters who turned out in their droves to show their gratitude to Warnock and his players and hopefully see them pick up a point or three on home turf for the final time in 2015/16.

Disappointingly, they slipped to a 1-0 defeat to Blackburn, with Shane Duffy's sixth-minute header from a corner the only goal of the game as Rotherham signed off at the New York Stadium. It was a 'sloppy' goal to concede and there were elements of the performance that were somewhat 'sluggish', according to Warnock's post-match assessment.

Blackburn would be looking to go in a new direction in 2016/17 after it was announced that manager Paul Lambert would leave the Lancashire club at the end of the term. Similarly, the next order of business for the Millers was who would be in the dugout next season. There were calls to tie down Warnock to a new contract, with his existing short-term agreement running until the end of the current campaign, but, for now, they could soak up what they had achieved.

'I think it's dotting the i's and crossing the t's and we'll sail through that,' Rotherham chairman Tony Stewart reassured fans in the aftermath of the Wolves game which sealed the club's Championship survival. 'We're in serious talks and I think that we'll develop the talks, and I think there's a strong chance that Neil will be with us next season. He has enjoyed the stay with us. I think he wants to stay with us and we want to stay with him.'

The team took to the field for a lap of honour as Warnock thanked both sets of fans, who clapped him and his players off the pitch in a show of mutual respect. Nothing but pride remained for the team who defied the odds and proved just about everybody wrong in living to fight another day in the Championship. It was an 'emotional' moment for Warnock and, as it happened, it would be the last time the fans would see him in the home dugout at the New York.

'You wouldn't write us off against anyone in this league now and that is a sign of how far we have come. People know they are in for a tough game against us,' he reflected on the achievement after the game.

As the excitement began to die down when the fans filtered out of the ground, the players dusted off their finery ready for the end-of-season awards do. The arrival of Warnock transformed what was shaping up to be a season to sweep under the carpet into one of their most memorable Championship campaigns. There was plenty to celebrate that evening at the New York Stadium, despite the day's result against Blackburn, which you could turn a blind eye to, all things considered.

There was a clear winner in the running for the coveted player of the year award. Lee Camp made 42 appearances in all competitions, keeping 13 clean sheets in the process and, without his contribution since signing for the club in September – something of a parting gift from former boss Steve Evans – the Millers would have been down and out. The keeper went toe-to-toe with Lee Frecklington and Kirk Broadfoot for the accolade, but Camp won out. The stopper made it a double later in the evening when he collected the players' player of the year award – as decided by his team-mates – with Broadfoot coming a close second and Frecklington and Joe Mattock sharing third place in the rankings.

Meanwhile, Grant Ward had the young player of the year award in one hand and the goal of the season prize in the other to take back to his parent club, Tottenham Hotspur. The 21-year-old made 43 appearances across all competitions for the Millers as he made his Championship debut and, after a slow start to the season, took to the division like a duck to water. Rotherham academy graduate Jerry Yates and striker Jonson Clarke-Harris also staked a claim to the young player prize, but Ward came out on top.

The Spurs youngster's strike against Burnley back in October won the goal of the season. The award went to a vote, with Ward's thunderbolt in a 2-1 defeat to the Clarets, screened live on Sky Sports, seeing off Matt Derbyshire's chip against Bristol City and Mattock's strike from range against Brentford.

Frecklington was also recognised as the club's community player of the year for his efforts off the pitch. The Rotherham skipper, who stepped into the role of club captain in September, continued to dedicate himself to the cause away from what was happening on the field.

Saturday, 7 May 2016
KC Stadium
EFL Championship
Hull City 5 (Snodgrass 25', Hernandez 27', Livermore 40', 59', Diame 42')
Rotherham United 1 (Frecklington 16')
Before the Millers boarded the bus to East Yorkshire, a cheque was presented to Warnock by a group of Rotherham fans who had raised over £1,000 for a charity of his family's choosing. It was later donated to Cancer Research on behalf of Warnock's wife, Sharon, who was diagnosed with breast cancer in 2015. Hundreds of Millers fans dug deep to show their appreciation for Sharon, who encouraged her husband to take up the role at Rotherham when Tony Stewart picked up the phone at the beginning of February.

In return, she penned an open letter to supporters, which was issued via the club's official website. She thanked the club for giving their family 'something else to focus on other than this hiccup' in their lives.

'Please understand my humour when I tell you that my husband's only real talent lies in football management and I could count on one hand the amount of dinners he's made in 26 years,' she wrote in her address. 'I even resorted to giving a gift at Christmas of a cookery course designed for men.'

She confessed to 'slightly falling out of love with football' and 'the whole money-obsessed players, inflated egos, the clipboard management', instead preferring 'the old school football' of 'blood and guts, massive hearts, humour'.

'I am ridiculously proud of Neil and the way he manages,' she continued in her letter. 'It doesn't matter that he is useless at cooking, cleaning, washing, ironing and a million other things, because to see him on a training ground and hear him motivate his lads is unbelievable.

'Rotherham has given Neil a bunch of lads who have given him everything and then some. It was a perfect combination. Please thank everyone for all their generosity and support. You are a fabulous club and have played such a happy part in our life. You should all be very proud of yourselves.'

Just 90 minutes of the season was all that remained. Rotherham would soon have closure on their campaign. When Warnock named his team to face Hull City, there were seven changes from the side that Steve Evans fielded nine months earlier in the season's opener against MK Dons. Kelle Roos, Danny Collins, Aidy White, Tom Thorpe, Matt Derbyshire, Joe Newell and Chris Maguire were replaced by Lee Camp, Kirk Broadfoot, Richard Wood, Stephen Kelly, Frazer Richardson, Lee Frecklington and Jonson Clarke-Harris. Only Greg Halford, Grant Ward, Richie Smallwood and Danny Ward remained from the starting XI against MK Dons in August.

Warnock also saw the game as an opportunity to give academy youngster Darnelle Bailey-King a run-out. The youngster got some valuable minutes under his belt in the Championship when he was introduced in the latter stages of the game.

When Rotherham took the lead with 16 minutes played, Frecklington scoring his fifth goal of the season, it looked as though it was going to be their day. Grant Ward's cross from the right was cleared only as far as Smallwood, who nodded it down for his midfield partner to beat Allan McGregor on the turn and make it 1-0 to the Millers. It was an advantage that didn't last long. The Tigers scored four times in 17 minutes to stun Warnock's men, who switched off on the final day.

Robert Snodgrass made it 1-1 with an emphatic finish into the top corner around ten minutes after Rotherham opened the scoring. With just under half an hour on the watch, Hull's leading marksman, Abel Hernández, hit the 20-goal milestone with an acrobatic overhead kick to turn it around for the Tigers. Jake Livermore added to the growing scoreline, making it 3-1 with five minutes of the first half remaining. And just two minutes later, Senegal international Mohamed Diamé raced through on goal to add a fourth. At half-time, Rotherham trailed Hull, who had already secured a top-six finish, 4-1.

Around 15 minutes after the restart, the Tigers capped off a five-star performance as Snodgrass and Livermore combined to make it 5-1. From a routine straight off the training ground, Snodgrass flicked the ball on to Livermore, who grabbed his second goal of the game.

Warnock admitted that his side 'lost the plot', although he reiterated that his players shouldn't be judged on that performance. However, it meant that Hull were full of confidence heading into the play-offs. The Millers finished the season in 21st place, nine points clear of the drop after slipping two places from 19th on the back of consecutive defeats to Blackburn and Hull. Nevertheless, it was mission accomplished for Warnock, who left the club in a much better place than he found it – as was always his aim from the get-go – regardless of the afternoon's outcome.

'Once safety is guaranteed, it's normal for some players to switch off,' Smallwood explains. 'That maybe had something to do with it. If we weren't safe already, I don't think we would've [switched off] in that last game.'

Some suggested that the Millers were suffering from a hangover when that record-equalling 11-game run stretching back to February came to an end against Blackburn, but it didn't take away from how far they had come under Warnock.

Derbyshire recalls: 'I remember thinking, "Why are we celebrating staying up?" After we looked at the situation itself, it was probably a bigger achievement than actually getting promoted to the Championship. I'd rather finish on a high than start on a high.

'I never really looked at the situation as us fighting to stay in the league. I knew I was at a club where the main thing was to stay up and anything better than that would be an amazing achievement, but we took every game as it came because I knew we had a good squad and I thought we could do a lot more. Looking back on the great escape, as they say, it's an unbelievable achievement – it really is.'

League table:

Position	*Club*	*Pl*	*GD*	*Pts*
20	Fulham	46	-13	51
21	Rotherham United	46	-18	49
22	Charlton Athletic	46	-40	40
23	MK Dons	46	-30	39
24	Bolton Wanderers	46	-40	30

Warnock just missed out on back-to-back manager of the month awards. The Millers boss was nominated alongside Brighton & Hove Albion's Chris Hughton, Middlesbrough's Aitor Karanka and Brentford's Dean Smith after Rotherham registered just one defeat in seven league games in April. The prize went to Hughton, whose Brighton side won five of their six fixtures and Warnock – who claimed the accolade in March – couldn't have any complaints. Meanwhile, Halford was also up for the PFA player of the month award for April after scoring two important goals, including the winner against Leeds United and a goal against Huddersfield Town – two results which helped Rotherham to achieve safety.

Elsewhere, Burnley were crowned champions of the division, with Middlesbrough the runners-up, to secure automatic promotion back to the Premier League. It was Rotherham's final day opponents, Hull City, who joined them, winning promotion via the play-offs. The Tigers saw off Derby County in the semi-final before beating Sheffield Wednesday 1-0 in the final. At the other end of the table, Charlton Athletic, MK Dons and Bolton Wanderers were relegated to League One as the curtain came down on another enthralling season in English football.

Chapter Ten

The Aftermath

DESPITE THE fact that Rotherham United had only just closed the book on the 2015/16 campaign, there was little time to waste when it came to planning for the future, particularly given that there was still a question mark over who would be the club's manager come the beginning of the new term. After a turbulent season during which – even excluding caretaker managers – the Millers had gone through three different bosses, they needed some stability. That would only come from the reassurance that there was a new manager in place ready for the 2016/17 season – one that could pick up where Neil Warnock had left off and carry the club forward. For that reason, the man himself was the perfect fit and there had been some encouraging signs on that front. Warnock hadn't been backward in coming forward when expressing just how much he had enjoyed his time at Rotherham. Not to mention he was full of praise for chairman Tony Stewart, who he described as 'Mr Rotherham'.

Similarly, it was no secret that Rotherham wanted Warnock to stay on for another year, if not longer. Given what he'd achieved, pulling off the so-called great escape, there was a suggestion that the club could have been promotion contenders under Warnock. There was no telling what he could do if he was given a full season at the helm.

In his programme notes for the last home game of the season against Blackburn Rovers, after Rotherham had confirmed their place in the Championship for another season, Warnock explained: 'From day one when I came here, the chairman and I always said we would talk about the possibilities for next season if and when we were safe, and that's what we plan to do over the next week or so.'

On 12 May, conversations took place between Warnock and Stewart, which were described as 'positive', and it was thought that the day's discussions could be decisive in reaching a resolution. Stewart was expecting a final yes or no from the boss early the following week as fans eagerly checked in on social media to see what the verdict was to be. But a week later, it was confirmed that he would part company with the Millers.

A club statement read: 'Following lengthy and protracted discussions over the past two weeks, Rotherham United can confirm that Neil Warnock will not be the manager of the club going forward.

'We would like to place on record our thanks to Neil and his support staff for the 16 games that they led the team at the end of the 2015/2016 campaign, and wish Neil, Kevin Blackwell and Ronnie Jepson health and happiness for the future. We will be looking to release details of a new managerial appointment in due course.'

In the aftermath of the announcement, Warnock explained that he came close to penning a new deal. He'd caught the bug on the back of his stint at Rotherham and if not with the South Yorkshire club, he was eager to stay in management. After watching the play-offs – which saw Hull City, Barnsley and AFC Wimbledon all promoted from their respective leagues – he was reminded that there is nothing quite like it. Come the same time next season, he realised that was where he wanted to be and the idea of adding a record-breaking eighth promotion to his CV prompted a change of heart.

'Up until a couple of days ago, I thought I was staying,' he said at the time. 'I've been in talks with two or three others clubs and Tony [Stewart] knows about that. Leaving this club is one of the hardest decisions I've ever had to make. I love everything about it – the chairman, the people, the fans, the family feel. I understand the chairman's need for a quick decision and the time is right for both parties to go their separate ways. There'll always be the memory of what we achieved together.

'Had I stayed, I think it would have been for the wrong reasons, really. Up until a couple of days ago, I thought I was staying. Rotherham is a project and I want only one more year. They need someone to come in for two or three years, build things up bit by bit, consolidate their place in the Championship and then look to go on from there.'

Warnock explained that, had he been ten years younger, he would have had no qualms about signing a long-term deal with the club. He might have been the club's shortest-serving manager at the time of his departure, but he had made an impact. His decision to turn down the club's contract offer allowed Rotherham plenty of time to identify who would lead them into battle in the 2016/17 season and Warnock was a believer that, with a couple of additions in the summer transfer window, the club could consolidate their place in the Championship during the following campaign and kick on from there.

Behind the scenes, in amidst all the will-he-won't-he whisperings, Warnock had been working on contract negotiations. While the club has spent the most part of its recent history oscillating between League One and the Championship, it has sparked some debate as to whether fans would rather see their team riding high in the third tier or scraping by in the second division of English football. In the lower league, Rotherham have been a force to be reckoned with, winning football matches on a regular basis, creating a feelgood factor around the club. However, as was the case in the summer of 2016 when the season ended and the transfer window later opened for business, staying in the Championship gave them a fighting chance of holding on to their assets.

When the retained and released list was published, it was confirmed that 11 players would leave the New York Stadium upon the expiration of their contacts. Those players were Frazer Richardson, Lewis Buxton, Danny Collins, Lloyd Doyley, Adam Collin, Paddy Kenny, Alex Cairns, Paul Green, Emmanuel Ledesma, Jerome Thomas and Luciano Becchio.

It saw Collin leave the club after three years in South Yorkshire, during which time he added a League One promotion to his CV with the Millers. The keeper – signed from Carlisle United in the summer of 2013 – established himself as Evans's first-choice stopper as Rotherham won promotion via the play-offs. He maintained his 100 per cent record in penalty shoot-outs when it came down to spot kicks in the final.

'It was a little bit disappointing how it went,' he recalls. 'While I was in Aberdeen, the managers changed and Neil Warnock had come in. The two years previous, I'd had a fantastic time at the club and built some fantastic relationships up with the fans, the players and the staff. The rest of the time I look back on with hugely fond memories.'

Both Green and Richardson's two-year stays at the club came to an end, with ex-Doncaster Rovers midfielder Green playing 65 times and experienced former Premier League defender Richardson clocking up 43 appearances in all competitions. Buxton and Collins also departed after a single season, having played their parts in a memorable campaign.

Ledesma – who didn't look quite the same player he once had been – was released after rejoining the club in the summer following a successful loan stint in 2014/15 from Middlesbrough. Becchio, Thomas and Doyley, who played a handful of games between them, moved on at the end of the season, while goalkeeping duo Cairns and Kenny left without making an appearance.

A further ten players were still under contract. Those were Lee Camp, Joe Mattock, Lee Frecklington, Danny Ward, Greg Halford, Jonson Clarke-Harris, Joe Newell, Tom Thorpe, Aymen Belaïd and Richie Smallwood.

Kirk Broadfoot, Matt Derbyshire, Richard Wood, Leon Best and Stephen Kelly were all in talks with the club regarding their futures. In the end, Broadfoot inked a new two-year deal in late June, despite rumoured interest from elsewhere in the Championship, after Alan Stubbs was named as the new Millers manager.

Broadfoot explains: 'I had offers to go elsewhere that summer. I could've gone to Preston at the time, but we were settled and I really enjoyed it at the club. I was hoping Neil stayed on because I thought we could've done something special. Apart from playing for the team I supported growing up, Rotherham has been my best time in football by a mile. It was one of the best times I had in my football career.'

Rotherham called time on Derbyshire's stint with the Millers, with the club releasing a statement to clarify that he would be relocating to Cyprus to sign for AC Omonia Nicosia.

'The club would like to place on record that striker Matt Derbyshire left the club following the end of his contract,' the statement read. 'The player did not, as reported, reject a new contract. Rotherham United acknowledged the effort and professionalism from Matt during his time with the Millers, but the club took the decision not to give him a new contract.'

Despite being sent out on loan twice during the season, Wood – who was out of the picture prior to Warnock's arrival – penned a new one-year deal in what he described as a 'straightforward' decision and for the future club captain, the rest is history. Likewise, Kelly took up the club's offer of an extension, with the Republic of Ireland international signing to remain a Millers player until the end of the 2016/17 season.

Leon Best departed upon the expiry of his short-term deal after helping the Millers to achieve their goal of survival by chipping in with four hugely important goals in 16 appearances. The striker was subsequently taken on trial by Ipswich Town, impressing the Tractor Boys enough to earn a contract.

The most exciting news coming out of the New York Stadium in the close season was the announcement that captain Lee Frecklington, who still had a year to run on his existing deal, had been rewarded with a new contract which would last until the end of 2017/18. The midfielder, who was handed the armband midway through the season, was as good as any new signing for the club. Frecklington joined Rotherham from Peterborough United in January 2013 on a permanent deal on the back of a successful loan spell, going on to achieve back-to-back promotions with the Millers. And the good news was that he wasn't going anywhere any time soon.

Frecklington recalls: 'That's one of the reasons I speak of Neil so highly. I wasn't actually out of contract that year, so I wasn't expecting a new contract, but he came to me and said, "You deserve one." I feel for somebody to do that when they don't have to do it, I respected him so much. I thought, "You know what, that's amazing."' When we went away that summer, I was really hoping that he was going to take the job permanently.'

* * *

After Warnock's exit was announced, it didn't take long for clubs to begin to circle. In the time between leaving Rotherham and taking up the role at Cardiff City, his name was linked with the likes of Aston Villa, Derby County and Blackburn Rovers. All three clubs were without managers, with Villa ending 2015/16 with former Rotherham interim boss Eric Black in charge on a temporary basis. If anything, it showed just how lucky the Millers were to have had Warnock, if only for 16 games, with the ex-Rotherham boss now being considered by top-end Championship clubs on the back of what he'd achieved in South Yorkshire.

Just over two months into the new season, Paul Trollope's departure from Cardiff City – after just 12 games in charge – paved the way for Warnock's return to the dugout in October 2016, having been out of work since his contract expired at Rotherham in May. He'd bided his time and waited for the right opportunity before the Bluebirds became his 15th different club. However, promotion number eight was on the back burner for the time being. It was still early days but, with Cardiff sitting second-bottom of the Championship when Warnock arrived in Wales, he admitted himself that it might be too much of an ask for 2016/17. But – as Rotherham found out – you can never rule out a Neil Warnock team. After posting a respectable 12th-place finish that season, he was true to his word the following campaign.

Meanwhile, the Millers had chosen Alan Stubbs as their new manager, with Stubbs leaving Scottish Premiership outfit Hibernian to take up his first job in England. The former Bolton Wanderers, Celtic and Everton defender had big shoes to fill – as would whoever succeeded Warnock. By mid-October, Rotherham were rock bottom of the Championship, with Stubbs having won just one of his 13 league games. On a barren run of six straight defeats and with their season falling apart, the club decided it was time for a change and Stubbs was dismissed.

In February 2017, Rotherham came up against Warnock for the first time since his exit when Cardiff hosted the Millers. The Bluebirds thrashed Rotherham, who were managed by interim boss Paul Warne. The former fitness coach, who made just shy of 300 appearances for the club as a player over two spells, stepped up after Kenny Jackett lasted just 39 days in charge before quitting. When the final whistle blew to put the Millers out of their misery, a 5-0 win for Warnock's Cardiff – the club's biggest victory in seven years – should have delighted the Bluebirds boss, but he admitted afterwards it was a poignant moment and he 'didn't feel good about the game' with it being his 'old club'.

However, he had nothing but admiration for his opposite number, who had taken up the role on a caretaker basis under equally unappetising circumstances. Warne was somebody Warnock had worked with during his brief time at the club, when he was part of the backroom staff. In an interview with the *Yorkshire Post* in December 2020, while in charge of Middlesbrough, Warnock explained that he was 'absolutely delighted' when Warne took the job on a permanent basis, reminiscing about the first time he met the former fitness coach.

Warnock – talking about Warne, whose Rotherham side were struggling once more in the Championship in 2020/21 – recalled: 'I remember saying to Blackie and Ronnie, "Bloody hell, I like him, I can trust him." I think this is "his" job and I keep saying to Tony [Stewart] when they do have a few bad results "Don't get silly, Tony" because Warney is a gem of a lad and he cares.' Warnock was still looking out for the club from afar.

But in 2016/17, Rotherham were rooted to the bottom of the table on 17 points, having been 14 adrift of safety when they went up against their former boss. Not even a Warnock special could save them now. The Millers became the first team in the top six tiers of English football to suffer relegation that season after three years in the Championship. In the summer, as they prepared to regroup ahead of a promotion push, Warnock raided his former team for some of his old favourites. Greg

Halford had already joined him in Wales in the January 2017 transfer window and Warnock poached goalkeeper Lee Camp and forward Danny Ward – Rotherham's top scorer in 2016/17 – ahead of the 2017/18 season, with the club unable to hold on to the pair in League One.

Warnock was tied with Dave Bassett, Graham Taylor and Jim Smith on seven promotions as a manager, but he was about to overtake the trio. The Bluebirds were runners-up to champions Wolverhampton Wanderers as they sealed automatic promotion back to the Premier League. Warnock claimed a record-breaking eighth promotion in the process – more than any other manager in English football. Going hand-in-hand, the good times returned for Rotherham. The Millers bounced back to the Championship at the first time of asking, beating Shrewsbury Town in the League One play-off final at Wembley. It was raw eggs and sherry – the tipple Warnock famously used to make his players drink as a pre-match beverage back in his early management days – all around.

* * *

Rotherham and Warnock have crossed paths on more than one occasion since then. In November 2021, the legendary manager – having joined Middlesbrough after leaving Cardiff – took charge of his 1,602nd match in management to set a new record for the most games managed in English football. The Millers had, by that time, embraced their reputation as a yo-yo club, with a further two promotions from League One and two relegations from the Championship. One of those promotions came during a COVID-curtailed campaign in 2019/20 when the standings were determined by points per game, before they embarked on a double-winning season in 2021/22 which included an EFL Trophy win at Wembley and automatic promotion from League One as the roller-coaster ride continued. It coincided with Warnock officially announcing his short-lived retirement from management in April 2022 after 42 years in the job, although there were some raised eyebrows from those who weren't quite sure whether to take him seriously. Upon the news, he spoke fondly of his time at Rotherham, looking back on the great escape as his finest hour at the time.

Speaking to Sky Sports, he said: 'I thought my biggest achievement was not even a promotion. It was keeping Rotherham in the Championship when we were six points adrift with 16 games to go and eight out of the top nine clubs to play. We went on a fabulous run. What a great group of boys they were. They were limited in certain attributes, but we got them believing in themselves.'

However, nobody was fooled and his decision to come out of retirement for another of his former clubs, Huddersfield Town, in February 2023 came as little surprise. The Terriers were seven points adrift in March. At a similar stage of the season when he was at Rotherham, it was all coming together for Warnock. So for Huddersfield, it was a desperate situation which looked beyond repair, but it still wasn't enough to put him off. For the likes of ex-Millers striker Danny Ward, who was on the books at Huddersfield at the time, memories resurfaced of some seven years earlier when Warnock rode in on a white horse to come to Rotherham's rescue. The fact that he had been there and done it with Rotherham gave the Terriers hope that he could pull off the impossible twice.

Indeed, he was up to his old tricks again as the West Yorkshire team finished in 18th place come the end of the campaign, securing safety with a game to spare. It was hardly a surprise, given what he'd achieved at Rotherham, that he'd done it again. Huddersfield ended the season three points ahead of Rotherham, who finally broke the cycle to remain in the Championship under boss Matt Taylor – one of just five managers to have kept the Millers in the second tier since

1980, alongside Emlyn Hughes, Ronnie Moore, Steve Evans and, of course, Warnock.

He didn't seem to need much convincing to commit to another year with Huddersfield, either. Since walking away from a new deal with the Millers at the end of the 2015/16 season, one more year had become two and then three and so on.

Rotherham and Warnock came face-to-face once again during the 2023/24 campaign for a Yorkshire derby in the Championship and, ever Rotherham's biggest cheerleader, Warnock talked about the 'typical bread and butter club' as a 'special' place, affirming: 'It's the type of club that I love.'

It was no great shock, then, that when the Millers found themselves in the market for a new manager at the tail end of 2023, there were calls for Warnock – who had begun to liken himself to the famous American oil well firefighter, Red Adair – to consider a second stint in charge. However, he ruled himself out on the basis that he was only looking for a short-term fix.

Rotherham and Warnock were a match made in heaven right from the start. Everyone associated with the South Yorkshire club hoped that they would get to keep the boss for a little longer but it's evident that, for both parties, the memory of those three-and-a-bit months they spent together still lingers.

Had he opted to turn down the Millers and remain in the land of beautiful beaches and Cornish pasties – and who could've blamed him – would it have altered the trajectory of Warnock's and the club's paths? We'll never know, but his decision certainly made Rotherham's time in the Championship all the more entertaining. And as accustomed as both Rotherham and Warnock have become to the highs and lows of English football, it's safe to say they wouldn't have it any other way.

Chapter Eleven

What Came Next?

ALMOST A decade has passed since Neil Warnock swept through South Yorkshire and saved Rotherham United's season in a whirlwind three months. A lot has happened in the intervening period for everyone involved. For some, it marked their last season in red and white as they moved on to pastures new, like Warnock himself, while others stuck around the New York Stadium for a while longer. Here is a look at what came next for some of those key characters that starred in the great escape of 2015/16.

Neil Warnock

Cardiff City became Warnock's next club in October 2016 after leaving Rotherham at the end of the 2015/16 campaign. He added a record-breaking eighth promotion to his CV with the Bluebirds the following season when he guided the Welsh club back to the Premier League. He then went on to manage Middlesbrough where he surpassed the 1,600-game mark before announcing his retirement in April 2022. However, just ten months later, he overturned his decision as he stepped out to take charge at Huddersfield Town – another of his former clubs, having managed them between 1993 and 1995 – and he saved the Terriers from relegation. The veteran boss tried his hand in Scotland with Aberdeen as the club's interim manager before becoming an advisor at non-league Torquay United.

Kevin Blackwell

After helping Neil Warnock pull off the great escape at Rotherham, his assistant, Kevin Blackwell, followed him to Cardiff City and, later, Middlesbrough. He left Boro along with Warnock and Ronnie Jepson when the trio stepped down in November 2021. Blackwell then had a spell managing Nakhon Ratchasima in Thailand's top flight before being appointed as the technical director at Lechia Gdańsk, a club who competed in and won Poland's second tier.

Ronnie Jepson

Similarly, Ronnie Jepson linked up with Neil Warnock and Kevin Blackwell at Cardiff and Middlesbrough. When Warnock came out of retirement to help Huddersfield, he was joined by Jepson – who played for the Terriers between 1993 and 1996 – as his assistant coach. The pair pulled off yet another miracle before signing a new one-year contract with the club. And, in February 2024, Jepson followed Warnock up to Scotland for a brief spell in charge at Aberdeen.

Steve Evans

After eight months in charge at Elland Road, Steve Evans and his assistant Paul Raynor parted ways with Leeds United. Evans went on to manage Mansfield Town in League Two between November 2016 and February 2018 before moving on to Peterborough United. After a stint at League One Gillingham, Evans was appointed by Stevenage in March 2022. He kept the club – who were perched just above the relegation zone in League Two when he arrived – in the EFL in 2021/22 before guiding them to a second-place finish in 2022/23 to secure automatic promotion. As fate would have it, on 17 April 2024, Evans returned to Rotherham on a three-year deal, tasked with achieving an immediate return to the Championship.

Neil Redfearn

Neil Redfearn returned to management with Doncaster Belles in December 2017. The former Rotherham boss – who had been out of work since being sacked by the Millers in February 2016 – led them to their first trophy since 1994 before making the switch to Liverpool Women. During his time with Newcastle United's under-23s, Redfearn took charge of the first team as the club's caretaker following the departure of Rafael Benítez. The former Leeds United boss had a stint with Sheffield United Women before quitting in November 2022. He stepped in to help out one of his former clubs, Oldham Athletic, on a caretaker basis before moving on to a new role as a development coach at Bradford City.

Eric Black

After a brief stint in the hotseat at Aston Villa following the departure of boss Rémi Garde, Eric Black left the club in June 2016. He was named as Claude Puel's assistant at Southampton later that month before he stepped down in December 2017, citing personal reasons for his exit.

Nicky Eaden

Nicky Eaden's departure from Rotherham was announced following the appointment of Alan Stubbs. Eaden went on to work as a development coach at Coventry City before becoming assistant manager at Chesterfield. He managed a handful of non-league clubs and had a spell in Jamaica before returning to Barnsley as an academy coach.

Lee Camp

Keeper Lee Camp joined up with Neil Warnock once again at Cardiff City in the summer of 2017. The stopper, who hadn't played for the Millers since November 2016 after picking up an injury towards the end of his stay in South Yorkshire, signed a two-year contract with the Bluebirds. He made 12 appearances in the Championship on loan with Sunderland in 2017/18. The former Northern Ireland international went on to have spells at the likes of Championship Birmingham City and League One Swindon Town, with his last club being National League side Wrexham, who were purchased by Hollywood duo Ryan Reynolds and Rob McElhenney in November 2020.

Adam Collin

One of Rotherham's Wembley-winning heroes, Adam Collin, departed the club at the end of 2015/16, having spent time on loan with Aberdeen during the season. After two years at Notts County, he rejoined Carlisle United – the team with whom he won the EFL Trophy back in 2011 – for a second spell. After scooping the club's player of the season award for 2018/19, the keeper dropped down into non-league before announcing his retirement in December 2021. In November 2022, he joined Mansfield Town's coaching set-up as the Stags' head of goalkeeping as he turned his attentions to life after his playing career.

Kelle Roos

Despite an underwhelming loan spell at Rotherham, Kelle Roos eventually established himself as Derby County's first-choice stopper in the Championship after a series of loan spells with the likes of AFC Wimbledon, Bristol Rovers, Port Vale and Plymouth Argyle. Most notably, he helped the Wombles win promotion in the 2016 League Two play-off final against Plymouth. He made his league debut for the Rams in January 2019 and, after eight years with the club, Roos signed for Scottish Premiership side Aberdeen upon the expiry of his deal, before relocating to Italy to sign for Serie C side Triestina.

Lewis Buxton

Midway through the 2015/16 season, Lewis Buxton waived a clause in his contract which would see the full-back trigger an extension to his deal and, at the end of the campaign, he was released after a year with Rotherham. The following summer, the former Sheffield Wednesday man signed a one-year deal with recently relegated Bolton Wanderers in League One, making 11 appearances as the Trotters won promotion back to the Championship. At the end of the campaign, Buxton hung up his boots for good.

Danny Collins

Having made 26 appearances for Rotherham as they secured Championship survival, experienced defender Danny Collins became a free agent at the end of the season. He signed a short-term deal with League Two side Grimsby Town in September 2016. Collins remained with the Mariners for three years, becoming a mainstay in the side before calling time on his career in December 2019 after being released by Grimsby following the conclusion of the 2018/19 season.

Kirk Broadfoot

Kirk Broadfoot returned later to his native Scotland after leaving Rotherham in the summer of 2017. He had subsequent spells in the Scottish Premiership with Kilmarnock and St Mirren – the club he joined as a 17-year-old and who he went on to captain, making over 170 appearances in his first stint – before dropping down to the Championship to sign for Inverness Caledonian Thistle. In June 2023 he signed a one-year deal with Greenock Morton, still going strong at the age of 40.

Richard Wood

After a season of uncertainty in 2015/16, Richard Wood opted to stay put at the New York Stadium and went on to write himself into the club's history books. In January 2018, the long-serving defender was appointed as the new club captain, inheriting the armband from the outgoing Lee Frecklington. Wood won three promotions with the Millers and registered two Wembley wins – one of which came in the 2018 League One play-off final and the other in the 2022 EFL Trophy Final. With more than 600 career appearances under his belt, Wood stepped in alongside Lee Peltier as caretaker manager following the exit of Paul Warne. He bade the club an emotional farewell at the end of the 2022/23 season to sign for local rivals Doncaster Rovers after nine memorable years with Rotherham.

Harry Toffolo

Loan spells in League One with Peterborough United, Scunthorpe United and Doncaster Rovers followed Harry Toffolo's spell at Rotherham. During the January transfer window of 2018, the former Norwich City man made a permanent move to Millwall but left without featuring for the Lions. However, Toffolo played every game for Lincoln City as they won promotion from League Two in 2018/19, being named in the division's PFA team of the year. He caught the eye of Championship side Huddersfield Town before earning a Premier League move to Nottingham Forest.

Farrend Rawson

Derby County loanee Farrend Rawson embarked on loans with Coventry City and Accrington Stanley after getting his first taste of professional football at Rotherham. In January 2018, the defender left the Rams to sign for Forest Green Rovers on a permanent deal. In the summer of 2020, he signed for Forest Green's League Two rivals Mansfield Town and, after two seasons, Rawson made the switch to League One side Morecambe before returning to Accrington.

Stephen Kelly

The Millers turned out to be former Republic of Ireland international Stephen Kelly's ninth and final club. Kelly made 15 appearances as Rotherham stayed up under Warnock, earning him a new deal. However, the defender, who started out at Tottenham Hotspur, called time on his playing career after remaining with the Millers for a further year in 2016/17.

Greg Halford

The dream team reunited at Cardiff City when Greg Halford signed for the Welsh club in January 2017. The following season, he played his part as the Bluebirds went up to the Premier League as the Championship's runners-up. Halford moved on to Scottish Premiership side Aberdeen in 2018/19 and, after a spell with Southend United in League Two, he made a switch to League of Ireland side Waterford. Halford has since spent time on the books of Billericay Town and Hashtag United in non-league.

Frazer Richardson

After two seasons with his hometown team, Rotherham United, Frazer Richardson made the short journey across the M1 to sign for League Two outfit Doncaster Rovers. The defender later extended his short-term agreement with Rovers but, after battling with injury, Richardson left the South Yorkshire club in December 2016.

Tom Thorpe

The 2016/17 season saw Tom Thorpe head out on loan to League One side Bolton Wanderers before leaving Rotherham at the end of the term. He linked up with Indian Super League team ATK to work under then-boss Teddy Sheringham. After five years out of the game, the defender made a return to football with non-league outfit Macclesfield and, later, Stalybridge Celtic.

Lee Frecklington

In January 2018, Rotherham and skipper Lee Frecklington – who switched to his hometown club Lincoln City, where he came through the ranks as a youngster – went their separate ways. He made 30 appearances – alongside Toffolo – in all competitions as the Imps were promoted from League Two in 2018/19. The double promotion winner, who gave his all in the red and white of Rotherham, signed for non-league Frickley Athletic, managed by his uncle, Dave Frecklington, for the 2021/22 season to prolong his playing career. Aged 36, he made the decision to hang up his boots for good.

Emmanuel Ledesma

Picked up by Brentford on non-contract terms after leaving Rotherham, Emmanuel Ledesma had spells with Greek Super League club Panetolikos, along with New York Cosmos and FC Cincinnati in America. Ledesma's next move took him to Finland to sign for Seinäjoen Jalkapallokerho and, after another stint in the USA, he joined Barnechea of the Chilean second tier. He later returned to the States to join Las Vegas Lights, a USL Championship team formed in 2017.

Paul Green

Following spells with EFL clubs Oldham Athletic and Crewe Alexandra after leaving Rotherham, Paul Green dropped into the semi-professional game with Boston United and Worksop Town. The former Republic of Ireland international also tried his hand at coaching as his playing career began to wind down, working with one of his former clubs, Doncaster Rovers, as part of the backroom staff.

Grant Ward

On the back of a memorable loan spell with the Millers, Grant Ward penned a three-year contract with Championship side Ipswich Town. The midfielder – who was linked with a move back to the New York Stadium in 2019 when Paul Warne was in charge – transferred to Blackpool after recovering from a cruciate knee ligament injury. In the January 2023 transfer window, he switched to League One side Bristol Rovers.

Richie Smallwood

Sent out on loan to Scunthorpe United by then-Rotherham boss Alan Stubbs in 2016/17, it would be Richie Smallwood's final season at the club. He signed for Blackburn Rovers, helping the club to win promotion back to the second tier – as he had done with Rotherham in 2013/14 – and cementing his status as a fan favourite at Ewood Park. Smallwood made it a third League One promotion with Hull City in 2020/21 before the former Tigers skipper joined League Two outfit Bradford City in the summer of 2022, where he was also named club captain.

Joe Newell

After Rotherham suffered relegation at the end of the 2016/17 campaign, Joe Newell chose to stick around and become a part of Paul Warne's Rotherham side that won the League One play-off final at Wembley to bounce back at the first time of asking the following year. Newell moved north of the border at the end of the 2018/19 season, going on to rack up over 100 appearances for Scottish Premiership team Hibernian. He also scooped both the club's player and players' player of the year accolades in 2022/23.

Danny Ward

During the summer of 2017, while Neil Warnock was getting the band back together at Cardiff City, the former Rotherham boss recruited Danny Ward. The striker – alongside former Millers team-mate Halford – went on to win promotion to the Premier League with Warnock. Rotherham received a seven-figure fee for the forward, who reached double figures during the 2016/17 season for the Millers. Ward, who netted his first Premier League goal against Arsenal for the Bluebirds, re-signed for Huddersfield Town – the club from which Rotherham signed him – ahead of the 2020/21 campaign. Under Warnock, the Terriers pulled off a great escape of their own in 2022/23 as Ward played his part once again.

Jonson Clarke-Harris

In January 2018, Jonson Clarke-Harris headed out on loan from Rotherham to Coventry City, with a view to making the move a permanent one. After helping the club win promotion from League Two, he inked a two-year deal with the Sky Blues. Clarke-Harris moved on to Bristol Rovers the following year and his prolific form for the Gas caught the eye of Peterborough United – one of his former clubs. In his first season back at London Road, he scooped the League One player of the year award and the Golden Boot as Posh clinched automatic promotion back to the Championship. In May 2024, it was announced that Clarke-Harris would rejoin Rotherham ahead of their 2024/25 League One campaign.

Matt Derbyshire

Having scored 17 goals in 69 league games in red and white, Matt Derbyshire joined Cypriot side Omonia Nicosia in the summer of 2016 after his contract expired with Rotherham. He spent four seasons playing for the club in the country's top tier, twice winning the division's Golden Boot before moving on to Australian A-League outfit Macarthur FC. A spell back in Cyprus with AEK Larnaca preceded a stint in the Indian Super League with NorthEast United, before Derbyshire returned to England to sign for League Two side Bradford City, where he was reunited with former Rotherham teammate Richie Smallwood.

Leon Best

At the conclusion of his contract with the Millers, Leon Best – one of the main protagonists in Rotherham's great escape – departed the New York Stadium despite holding negotiations with the club in the wake of the 2015/16 season. The striker went on to sign for Championship rivals Ipswich Town but after a single season at Portman Road, he was released. Charlton Athletic became Best's final club when he penned a short-term deal with the Addicks in November 2017 before his contract expired the following January.

Statistics

Pre-season results

Friendly	Wed 8 Jul 2015	Parkgate	0-6	**Rotherham**
Friendly	Sat 11 Jul 2015	Stocksbridge	0-3	**Rotherham**
Friendly	Tue 14 Jul 2015	Alfreton	3-2	**Rotherham**
Friendly	Sat 18 Jul 2015	Greenock	0-3	**Rotherham**
Friendly	Tue 21 Jul 2015	Dundee	0-1	**Rotherham**
Friendly	Sat 25 Jul 2015	Partick Thistle	1-1	**Rotherham**
Friendly	Wed 29 Jul 2015	**Rotherham**	1-2	Leicester
Friendly	Sat 1 Aug 2015	**Rotherham**	2-1	Mainz

2015/16 results

Championship	Sat 8 Aug 2015	**Rotherham**	1-4	MK Dons
League Cup	Tue 11 Aug 2015	**Rotherham**	1-0	Cambridge
Championship	Sat 15 Aug 2015	Nottm Forest	2-1	**Rotherham**
Championship	Tue 18 Aug 2015	**Rotherham**	0-0	Preston
Championship	Sat 22 Aug 2015	QPR	4-2	**Rotherham**
League Cup	Tue 25 Aug 2015	**Rotherham**	1-2	Norwich
Championship	Sat 29 Aug 2015	**Rotherham**	1-3	Fulham
Championship	Sat 12 Sept 2015	Charlton	1-1	**Rotherham**
Championship	Tue 15 Sept 2015	Brighton	2-1	**Rotherham**
Championship	Sat 19 Sept 2015	**Rotherham**	2-1	Cardiff
Championship	Sat 26 Sept 2015	Birmingham	0-2	**Rotherham**
Championship	Fri 2 Oct 2015	**Rotherham**	1-2	Burnley
Championship	Sat 17 Oct 2015	Brentford	2-1	**Rotherham**

Championship	Tue 20 Oct 2015	**Rotherham**	1-1	Reading
Championship	Fri 23 Oct 2015	**Rotherham**	1-2	Sheff Wed
Championship	Sat 31 Oct 2015	Derby	3-0	**Rotherham**
Championship	Tue 3 Nov 2015	Middlesbrough	1-0	**Rotherham**
Championship	Sat 7 Nov 2015	**Rotherham**	2-5	Ipswich
Championship	Sat 21 Nov 2015	Leeds	0-1	**Rotherham**
Championship	Sat 28 Nov 2015	**Rotherham**	3-0	Bristol City
Championship	Sat 5 Dec 2015	**Rotherham**	1-2	Wolves
Championship	Fri 11 Dec 2015	Blackburn	1-0	**Rotherham**
Championship	Tue 15 Dec 2015	Huddersfield	2-0	**Rotherham**
Championship	Sat 19 Dec 2015	**Rotherham**	2-0	Hull
Championship	Sat 26 Dec 2015	**Rotherham**	4-0	Bolton
Championship	Tue 29 Dec 2015	Fulham	4-1	**Rotherham**
Championship	Sat 2 Jan 2016	Preston	2-1	**Rotherham**
FA Cup	Sat 9 Jan 2016	Leeds	2-0	**Rotherham**
Championship	Tue 12 Jan 2016	**Rotherham**	2-0	Brighton
Championship	Sat 16 Jan 2016	**Rotherham**	0-3	QPR
Championship	Sat 23 Jan 2016	Cardiff	2-2	**Rotherham**
Championship	Sat 30 Jan 2016	**Rotherham**	1-4	Charlton
Championship	Sat 6 Feb 2016	Bolton	2-1	**Rotherham**
Championship	Sat 13 Feb 2016	**Rotherham**	0-0	Birmingham
Championship	Sat 20 Feb 2016	Burnley	2-0	**Rotherham**
Championship	Tue 23 Feb 2016	Reading	1-0	**Rotherham**
Championship	Sat 27 Feb 2016	**Rotherham**	2-1	Brentford
Championship	Sat 5 Mar 2016	Sheff Wed	0-1	**Rotherham**
Championship	Tue 8 Mar 2016	**Rotherham**	1-0	Middlesbrough
Championship	Sat 12 Mar 2016	**Rotherham**	3-3	Derby
Championship	Sat 19 Mar 2016	Ipswich	0-1	**Rotherham**
Championship	Sat 2 Apr 2016	**Rotherham**	2-1	Leeds
Championship	Tue 5 Apr 2016	Bristol City	1-1	**Rotherham**
Championship	Sat 9 Apr 2016	MK Dons	0-4	**Rotherham**
Championship	Sat 16 Apr 2016	**Rotherham**	0-0	Nottm Forest

Championship	Tue 19 Apr 2016	**Rotherham**	1-1	Huddersfield
Championship	Sat 23 Apr 2016	Wolves	0-0	**Rotherham**
Championship	Sat 30 Apr 2016	**Rotherham**	0-1	Blackburn
Championship	Sat 7 May 2016	Hull	5-1	**Rotherham**

Player statistics

	Appearances (Substitute)	**Goals**
Tony Andreu	10 (1)	2
Darnell Bailey-King	0 (1)	0
Brandon Barker	1 (3)	1
Luciano Becchio	0 (2)	0
Aymen Belaïd	4 (0)	0
Leon Best	10 (6)	4
Jordan Bowery	3 (5)	1
Kirk Broadfoot	32 (1)	1
Chris Burke	5 (0)	2
Lewis Buxton	20 (0)	0
Alex Cairns	0 (0)	0
Lee Camp	42 (0)	0
Jonson Clarke-Harris	20 (17)	6
Adam Collin	2 (0)	0
Danny Collins	23 (3)	2
Chris Dawson	0 (0)	0
Matt Derbyshire	30 (8)	8
Lloyd Doyley	3 (0)	0
Shay Facey	6 (0)	0
Lee Frecklington	28 (1)	5
Paul Green	15 (11)	1
Greg Halford	21 (2)	2
Luke Hyam	2 (3)	0

Stephen Kelly	13 (2)	0
Paddy Kenny	0 (0)	0
Emmanuel Ledesma	3 (5)	0
Chris Maguire	6 (9)	0
Joe Mattock	36 (0)	1
Joe Newell	31 (7)	5
Vadis Odjidja-Ofoe	4 (0)	1
Farrend Rawson	15 (1)	2
Frazer Richardson	15 (5)	0
Kelle Roos	5 (0)	0
Andrew Shinnie	1 (2)	0
Richie Smallwood	44 (1)	1
Jerome Thomas	3 (3)	0
Tom Thorpe	5 (2)	2
Harry Toffolo	6 (1)	0
Danny Ward	23 (13)	4
Grant Ward	35 (8)	2
Mason Warren	0 (0)	0
Aidy White	4 (6)	0
Richard Wood	13 (0)	0
Jerry Yates	0 (0)	0

Championship table

		P	*W*	*D*	*L*	*GD*	*Pts*
1	Burnley (C, P)	46	26	15	5	+37	93
2	Middlesbrough (P)	46	26	11	9	+32	89
3	Brighton & Hove Albion	46	24	17	5	+30	89
4	Hull City (P)	46	24	11	11	+34	83
5	Derby County	46	21	15	10	+23	78
6	Sheffield Wednesday	46	19	17	10	+21	74
7	Ipswich Town	46	18	15	13	+2	69
8	Cardiff City	46	17	17	12	+5	68
9	Brentford	46	19	8	19	+5	65
10	Birmingham City	46	16	15	15	+4	63
11	Preston North End	46	15	17	14	0	62
12	Queens Park Rangers	46	14	18	14	0	60
13	Leeds United	46	14	17	15	-8	59
14	Wolverhampton Wanderers	46	14	16	16	-5	58
15	Blackburn Rovers	46	13	16	17	0	55
16	Nottingham Forest	46	13	16	17	-4	55
17	Reading	46	13	13	20	-7	52
18	Bristol City	46	13	13	20	-17	52
19	Huddersfield Town	46	13	12	21	-11	51
20	Fulham	46	12	15	19	-13	51
21	**Rotherham United**	**46**	**13**	**10**	**23**	**-18**	**49**
22	Charlton Athletic (R)	46	9	13	24	-40	40
23	Milton Keynes Dons (R)	46	9	12	25	-30	39
24	Bolton Wanderers (R)	46	5	15	26	-40	30

Acknowledgements

JUST OVER ten years ago, I started up a blog about my beloved football club, Rotherham United. We'd just been promoted back to the Championship after winning the play-off final at Wembley (a day which still takes some topping). At the time, it was more of an outlet to rant or rave, depending on the outcome on any given weekend. A decade on, I've somehow written a whole book on the Millers but without more than a few people, it wouldn't have been possible.

First of all, I'd like to say a huge thanks to Jim Brailsford and Trevor Price for kindly allowing me to use some of the amazing pictures they took during the 2015/16 season as they travelled up and down the country to photograph the Millers, through the good times and the bad. They've captured those memorable moments – the famous victories, the last-minute goals, the celebrations – and brought them to life in this book.

It goes without saying that there wouldn't have been a book to write if not for everyone involved with the club that season, from the managers to the coaches, to the players. Back in 2021, I first had the idea of writing a book about the great escape and since then, I've had the privilege of speaking to a number of former players who gave up their time to share their stories and talk through some of their memories from that campaign.

So, thank you to Adam Collin, Danny Ward, Farrend Rawson, Grant Ward, Greg Halford, Joe Mattock, Joe

Newell, Jonson Clarke-Harris, Kirk Broadfoot, Lee Camp, Lee Frecklington, Matt Derbyshire, Richard Wood and Richie Smallwood.

Thank you, too, to Richard Wood for producing a foreword. I know that season was more of a prequel for him in his Rotherham career, but I'm delighted to have a modern-day club legend introduce the book.

It would have been difficult to write this book without those who covered that roller-coaster ride of a season and all the twists and turns along the way. Rob Staton, Paul Davis, Jonathan Veal and Joe Cawthorn were some of the experts who were much closer to the action at the time. I just enjoyed following their reporting, as I still do! It was also hugely helpful when doing my research to take a trip down memory lane by re-reading about and listening to the sounds of that season.

On that note, a thank you, too, to the club's head of communications Sam Todd for his assistance in passing on some contact details and phone numbers and helping out wherever he could.

I also need to show some appreciation to my friend Ryan Grant who I leaned on for his thoughts, opinions and any pointers during the writing process. He's read the whole book back to front – probably more than once – and he's not even a Rotherham fan!

All of my family and friends have encouraged me and supported me while I was working on this book and I'm especially grateful for that. And, of course, a thank you to my family for clubbing together and buying me my first-ever season ticket all those years ago to get me started on this journey!

And last but certainly not least, a big thanks to the whole team at Pitch Publishing for taking this project on and making my dream of writing a book about my football club a reality.

I've said it before, but I'll say it again, particularly in recent years, there hasn't been a dull moment in the life of a Rotherham United fan and that itself is something to be grateful for, I suppose!

Bibliography

Books:

Somerton, G. *Still United: The History of Rotherham United* (Harefield: Yore Publications, 2008)

Warnock, N. *Made in Sheffield: Neil Warnock – My Story* (London: Hodder & Stoughton, 2007)

Websites:

bbc.co.uk/sport
examinerlive.co.uk
leedsunited.com
offsiderulepodcast.com
saddlers.co.uk
skysports.com
thefa.com
themillers.co.uk
tntsports.co.uk
walesonline.co.uk

Newspapers:

Bristol Post
Daily Mail
Football League Paper
News Shopper
Rotherham Advertiser
Sheffield Star
Yorkshire Post

Programmes:
Rotherham United v Blackburn Rovers [30 April 2016]
Rotherham United v Brentford [27 February 2016]
Rotherham United v Huddersfield Town [19 April 2016]
Rotherham United v Leeds United [2 April 2016]
Rotherham United v Middlesbrough [8 March 2016]

Radio:
BBC Radio Sheffield